Beatles & Others

JANET MACLEOD TROTTER

Published by MacLeod Trotter Books

New paperback edition: March 2011

ISBN 978-0-9566426-5-3

www.janetmacleodtrotter.com

Janet MacLeod Trotter was brought up in the North East of England with her four brothers, by Scottish parents. She is a best-selling author of 16 novels, including the hugely popular Jarrow Trilogy, and a childhood memoir, BEATLES & CHIEFS, which was featured on BBC Radio Four. Her novel, THE HUNGRY HILLS, gained her a place on the shortlist of The Sunday Times' Young Writers' Award, and THE TEA PLANTER'S DAUGHTER was longlisted for the RNA Romantic Novel Award. A graduate of Edinburgh University, she has been editor of the Clan MacLeod Magazine, a columnist on the Newcastle Journal and has had numerous short stories published in women's magazines. She lives in the North of England with her husband, daughter and son. Find out more about Janet and her other popular novels at: www.janetmacleodtrotter.com

By Janet MacLeod Trotter

Historical:
The Jarrow Trilogy
The Jarrow Lass
Child of Jarrow
Return to Jarrow
The Durham Trilogy
Hungry Hills
The Darkening Skies
Never Stand Alone
The Tyneside Sagas
The Tea Planter's Daughter
The Suffragette
A Crimson Dawn
A Handful of Stars
Chasing the Dream
For Love & Glory
Scottish Historical Romance
The Beltane Fires

Mystery:
The Vanishing of Ruth
The Haunting of Kulah

Teenage:
Love Games
Short Stories:
Ice Cream Summer

**To the Fab Four - Donald, Torquil, Rory and Angus -
with much love.
And in fond memory of our parents, Sheila and Norman:
loving, supportive, funny and generous. Always with us.**

Norman has a very genuine enthusiasm for history which could not help but inspire any boy he might teach... He was quite exceptionally popular with his equals and his seniors, and has indeed a remarkable talent for friendship ...I hold a very high opinion of him as a man and as a friend, and 1 believe that any school will be fortunate to get him.

H. Allen, Fellow and Tutor in Modern History, Oxford University, 1948.

Sheila has just the qualities of modesty, sturdiness, reliability and good spirits which make her ideal for the position [of head of house] ...I want you to know how I value and trust her... I consider her most outstanding in her capacity for understanding and dealing with people... I think she is a real leader.

Miss Waller and Miss Popham, Cheltenham Ladies College, 1942.

Contents

Born With a Tartan Spoon in My Mouth   1
One of the Lads   5
Land of Boy   12
Casting Off   20
My Dad was Ringo Starr   32
'I Want Never Gets'   44
Road to the Isles   56
Pastry and the Devil   64
Picnics and Massacres   75
Orgies and Old Maid   87
Fairies, Ghosts and Donovan   96
Zizz-Zizz-Zizz and the Germans   109
Tigers and Yoga   114
From Pimlico to Carnaby Street   123

Born With a Tartan Spoon in My Mouth

'Hey Scotchie, chase us!
Hey Scotchie, where you from?
Haggis Land?
Hey Scotchie, you're on!'

January 1958. Snow storms turned the roads to porridge. A baby blanket of white blizzard wrapped around the North East of England and drifting snow harried the travellers on the old North Road. The MacLeod parents pressed on to Newcastle.

In the Princess Mary Maternity Hospital, my mother, the actress, was centre stage labouring over a fourth birth in front of an audience of medical students. The climactic scene was a full blood transfusion that saved my life. Argumentative from the start, I was rhesus positive to Sheila's rhesus negative.

Meanwhile my father was calming his nerves in The Shallows pub, nursing his pint to keep it warm. Norman had a right to be nervous. This didn't just mean his first girl child might die, it meant draining off her pure Scottish blood. Excluded from the performance, Norman arrived for the curtain call. Sheila, having done all the hard work, had to soothe her pacing husband, now inwardly fortified but still fretful.

'They're filling my daughter full of Sassenach blood!' Norman cried.

The doctors tried to access a vein in my head but ended up refilling me at the foot. I was presented to my parents with shaved head and affectionately nick-named Yul Brynner. I lived and we all went home, 15 miles south to Durham City. The legend grew that the MacLeods were rushing north to have their child born the right side of the Border, but the January snow had thwarted the plan. A kind colleague assured my father that blood had been flown specially from the Hebrides for baby Janet, so everyone relaxed.

As my hair grew back the colour of rusty claymore and the fresh blood pumped, thickened and settled into its new home, I grew up believing these creation myths. Our family doctor, with cold hands and warm smile, colluded.

'Scots have green blood,' Dr Chapman teased. 'You've green blood in your veins.'

At five years-old I caught some infection and had to go into hospital for a fortnight. Several blood samples were taken but, confusingly, they were always red. Obviously they were siphoning off the Sassenach stuff. This was reassuring as the green blood must have still been in there lining my veins.

There was Irish blood too. D'Estaire and Roberts on my father's side. Our

1

family provided a minor character in the great drama of Catholic Emancipation, for our ancestor D'Estaire was killed in a pistol duel by Daniel O'Connell the Irish leader. An Irish nurse, Bernadette, came to help look after me for a week or two after the birth. Her father had a portrait of O'Connell, wearing white gloves because he had killed a man and wouldn't take Mass with his bare hands. My ancestor pricking the conscience of O'Connell, spurring him on to greater justice for his fellow Catholics.

So I grew up as a Scot (with a dash of Irish) in the North-East of England and never doubted my identity (until years later I went to live in Scotland and was continually mistaken for being English). For no one has a fiercer sense of national pride than the ex-pat or second generation exile. Three of my four brothers were born in Edinburgh, the other one in Durham. We two, born on foreign soil, were all the more chauvinistic for it. We hungered for stories of our roots, wallowed in Scottish romanticism and still get nasty over national football and rugby.

It was the early Sixties: my brothers and I, we were wild thistles among the English, prickly proud to wear the kilt. EPs of Scottish country dance music and Andy Stewart records lay beside the large mahogany-veneered gramophone. In our English accents we were word perfect in *Donald Where's Yer Troosers?* and *Scottish Soldier*. We sang of the dying soldier among foreign green hills and saw the rounded hills and pit heaps of County Durham. They were not our land's hills; not the towering, jagged, misty mountains over the sea, not the heather-hiding, rock-scrambling, bog-squelching hills of the Isle of Skye that belong to my family and me.

1966: we watched in distress the film *Culloden*, black and white atrocity, showing brave sword-wielding Highlanders being gunned down by Redcoat government troops. To the blast of bagpipes and skirl of bullets, wave after tartan wave were scythed down like harvesting oats. William, Duke of Cumberland, unleashed his Hanoverian soldiers to butcher the fleeing men, cut the throats of barefoot children and burn the sheltering plaid of women. A way of life went up in smoke; Gaelic culture torched. I cried for my ancestors facing cannon with knives.

It was done in a documentary style and so 'real' that I would not be fobbed off with, 'It's only a film!'

'Are they not really dying?' I blubbered.

'No,' Mum assured. 'Faith's brother is one of the actors. He had to fall down, pretending to be dead, then get up and charge on again.'

This was some consolation, to think of the Highland army being constantly recycled. But I was shocked by the unfairness of it all - guns against swords, cannon versus running men in bare feet, well-clothed soldiers hunting down and murdering tartan fugitives. At eight, I did not have the words to describe the sense of injustice, but I felt it keenly, even if they were just acting. This was my first experience of Imperial Might being more than a little heavy-handed with the locals.

2

We learned that the Jacobites had a nickname for Butcher Cumberland; "Stinking Billy" instead of "Sweet William". I went howling back to school crying "Stinking Billy!" at any of the boys who called me Scotchie.

'Hey, Scotchie, chase us!

Hey, Scotchie, you're on!'

I took the bait, pursuing them with a roaring noise that I thought best imitated a claymore-wielding Highlander.

'Hey, Stinking Billies!'

If they got away, my ultimate threat was to shout, 'I'll get my biggest brother, Donald, onto you!'

'Donald Duck! Donald Duck!' they chanted, running away.

* * *

There were other Scottish traits that betrayed our origins. We referred to a large meat plate as an "ashette", the old Scot's word from the French assiette which echoed the Auld Alliance between Scotland and France. Hallowe'en was celebrated as well as Guy Fawkes.

One half-term, I remembered Mum gouging out eyes in turnip lanterns and candlelight glowing through gaping turnip mouths. The kitchen flickered a harvest-moon yellow. The cat yawned sharp dagger teeth; shadows inched closer. We ducked for bobbing apples in a plastic bowl; our full faces rose dripping and grinning.

Dad was a lover of Robert Burns' poetry. Sometimes it made him cry. He could recite the whole of *Tam O 'Shanter*. We were charmed by strange words, bewitched by Bums; skellums, blellums, warlocks, winnock-bunkers, cutty sark. The spell of language stilled our bobbing minds as we huddled closer in the smoky dark, our nostrils tickled by the acrid smell of turnip and singeing string.

The cautionary tale of the boozing Tarn who nearly got caught by witches, joined the canon of childhood folklore. *Sleeping Beauty*, *Wizard of Oz*, *Tarn O 'Shanter* - for years there were witches at the foot of my bed. They lurked on the borders of sleep, grinning and turnip-faced, waiting for me to stretch out my feet in the chilly sheets.

* * *

Regularly, we ate haggis and porridge. In winter-time, Dad circled the kitchen table at breakfast, eating his bowlful of steaming porridge on the move. What was he doing? Expecting a sudden raid? Very likely. We lived in a boarding school full of boys where he could be ambushed at any moment and called away to do battle with some rebel caught smoking or trying to escape. (Granny bought a hotplate to keep his abandoned food warm during these skirmishes).

3

He would circle the table once, kissing us all on the head. Then he circled again with porridge bowl in hand. No doubt this roaming around the table was a throwback to a time when Highlanders had to be alert to danger and eat on the hoof. To us it seemed perfectly normal. We carried on eating and ignored him.

A generation later, I bought a bag of oatmeal and brewed up porridge so my two young children would grow strong on it and learn Highland stealth.

'Ugh, I'm not eating that!' they yelped in disgust.

'You're putting salt in it!' cried the Health Police.

Slightly peeved, I began to pace the kitchen, bowl in hand.

'What are you doing?' my daughter Amy, then eight years-old, asked suspiciously.

'Er - just keeping an eye on the toast,' I lied, suddenly embarrassed at their catching me being alert to danger and eating on the hoof like my ancestors.

'Well, sit down, it's rude!' Amy said briskly.

I tried to explain. 'You see Granddad used to do it...'

'Well, Granddad does lots of crazy things,' she replied, 'it's okay for him.'

I sat down and pondered my cultural failure. Perhaps it was best if some traditions withered on the spoon.

One of The Lads

According to my mother, one of the first words I learned to say was, 'Boys'. My second speech development was 'Boys, boys!' There was good reason for this. Not only did I grow up with four brothers, but my first home was The Caffinites, a boarding house of Durham School, accommodating up to seventy schoolboys.

When my father had applied for a job teaching history there, my parents had got out the atlas to discover where Durham was. After three years, and the pleasant discovery that Durham was a picturesque cathedral city with a river, university and other migrant Scots, Dad was appointed housemaster of The Caffinites.

It was Norman who got the appointment and was in charge of the boys, but the school expected Sheila to be unpaid manager in charge of catering, domestic staff and a matron inherited from the previous regime. And just to prevent her lapsing into idleness, she had by then, two baby boys of her own to cope with. This was the 1950s. There was no crash course in catering or book-keeping given; it was just expected of housemasters' wives to take on the job. The headmaster, if it crossed his mind at all, no doubt thought that knocking up seventy fried eggs every morning came naturally to young women.

But Sheila was an actress by profession, trained at prestigious RADA in London and hooked on the smell of grease-paint not lard. Cooking up a storm on the stage, not in the kitchen, was her forte. She hated cooking. Unfortunately for her, she had married no gourmet either. Norman, a former Second World War sailor, had been famous below deck for his culinary spills rather than skills. He had seen action from Archangel to Alexandria, and he took no prisoners on the mess deck either. He confessed that his fried eggs were cooked to the consistency of rubber, which was good for economy, because one time, when he dropped them on the galley floor, he was able to pick them up unbroken and put them back on the tray ready to serve.

For years I wondered why naval officers referred to the braid on their cuffs denoting rank as "scrambled eggs". Could it be in fond memory of able-seamen like my father tipping breakfast over their uniforms? I like to think of Captain McGrath of *The Glengyle*, (Norman's first ship) gazing fondly at the gold braid on his sleeve and murmuring, 'Ah, North Africa landings - eggs up-side-down for breakfast - MacLeod on duty.'

I'm sure Sheila took no lessons from Norman on the art of egg cooking, but it does seem a bit of a coincidence that by the early 1960s, the school abolished in-house catering and set up a central dining hall for all the boarding houses.

Although Durham School had been in existence since medieval times, Caffinites was a solid pre-First World War, purpose-built boarding house of weathered stone and leaded window panes. It was softened by creepers around the main entrance and wore a neat collar of flowerbeds full of wallflowers. Dipping down in front were two strips of lawn divided by a rockery. On the east side, a third square of lawn outside the kitchen window had been appropriated by us kids for football and cricket. Its surface resembled one of those zoo pens for rhinos where all the grass has long been trampled into mudflats.

George Laws, the gentle gaunt-faced gardener, gave up trying to revive it, though it must have pained him to see such an eye-sore. But then George's fortitude had been forged years before. A soldier in the Second World War, he had been a Japanese POW, a survivor of the infamous Burma Railway. He always looked old, his tall thin frame stooped over a spade, his walk unhurried. Yet he must only have been in early middle-age. Captivity had robbed him of looking his age.

When George came and replaced Tom (who had been tough and tight-lipped and the unsentimental drowner of kittens), he had to put up with teasing from me and my schoolfriends. We would track him down and chant:

'Georgy-porgy, pudding and pie,
Kissed the girls and made them cry!
When the boys came out to play,
Georgy-porgy ran away!'

Then, giggling, we would scamper off in the hope we might be chased. But George would not be provoked and, laughing quietly, carried on working. A shy bachelor, he would in later years over glasses of Christmas beer, always ask me with a chuckle, 'Are you courtin' yet?'

George never married. Instead he nurtured the earth with his kindness and sunny nature. No bitter weeds grew in his garden and he never had a bad word to say about anyone - neither tyrant captors nor pestering girls.

Flanking the house on one side was a large vegetable garden with strawberry patch and gooseberry bushes, prettified by sweet-peas. On the other, screening Caffinites off from its twin rival Poole House (built to the exact same plan), was a clump of trees where we played on a climbing frame and watched the boys walking up the drive to their own side entrance.

Caffinites was close to a main road which meandered eccentrically around the school like a river that had lost its way, cutting off the boarding house from the bulk of school buildings, chapel and playing fields. Food, lessons, games and prayers lay a quick dash away down the drive and over the road at a blind corner. A barrier was erected to discourage the pupils from sprinting down the slope and into the path of lurking Morris Minors. Instead, this just encouraged them to run and jump, using it as a hurdle.

From the front, the house looked imposing under its heavy gables, behind neat flowerbeds and laburnum trees. At the back it was scuffed and untidy as a schoolboy; a hotch-potch of garages, coal heaps, fire-escapes and scrub. Ragged hedges of hawthorn and elderflower were the school boundary and below it, an easy scramble away, lay a democratic patchwork of allotments. Here, retired miners laboured in the daylight, cultivating the rich soil that had once lined a fishpond used by the medieval monks of Durham Abbey.

Beyond sat St Margaret's, the Victorian primary school to which I would go, with its asphalt yard and outside toilets, a comforting glance away from home. Further still, stretched the wilderness of Marjory Lane and St Margaret's churchyard, tossed together with terraced housing which clung onto rollercoaster slopes as they pitched down to the River Wear.

There were no high walls or barbed wire or searchlights dividing the two worlds; the private school from the republican gardening. They co-existed in mutual disinterest, each justified in being there since the days of the monks. To us (me-plus-a-brother or me-plus-a-friend) this unclaimed borderland was a place of adventure. Of no interest to the school gardeners, it was a fertile home for dens and lightening raids on the allotments to pick up rubbish - an old spoon, a medicine bottle, a streamer of used bus tickets - trophies to carry back to our squatters' camp.

We crept around the narrow network of paths like Peter Rabbit and Benjamin Bunny, thrilling at the thought of being spotted by some grumpy Mr McGregor who would tell us to 'Bugger off!' and send us scurrying for a gap under the hedge.

One time, when we had provoked such a reaction and scampered, squealing in excitement for the safety of our bolt hole, I slipped and fell into a generous pile of chestnut-coloured dog mess. It squelched under my palm, its foul stench released as it oozed between my fingers. I yelped in disgust. Rory (the brother nearest to me in age and so my constant companion and rival) laughed and ran on. Picking myself up and frantically wiping the sticky, nauseous mess onto the dirty verge, I ran after him protesting.

'It's not funny!' I shouted hotly, not sure if I was more indignant at the offending dog or my retreating brother. Of course, to a boy of eight it was hilarious. But it was one of those defining moments in my development. I grew up to be fascist about dog fouling. I became the sort of person who joined citizen action panels on dog fouling and confronted lazy dog owners with a demented gleam in my eye. They were not to know that each encounter forced me to re-live that moment where I was heading unstoppably towards my squelch with destiny.

* * *

Caffinites was divided into 'Our Side' and 'The Boys' Side'. Private versus Communal. We had bedrooms, they had dormitories. Our bathroom had one bath in it, their changing rooms had uninhibited rows of them. We lived at the front, they at the back, through swing doors.

On our side, rooms were light and spacious. The sitting-room and dining-room with their bay windows pulled off a certain elegance despite the wearing effects of five children. The floors were polished around fringed carpets and sun streamed into the large airy hallway. Coal fires kept them relatively warm in winter and a fire sometimes burned in the large nursery upstairs. Otherwise the only heating was from fat unlagged pipes that snaked up the stairs and along the corridors like the Lambton Worm.

I never remember being cold, but at times it must have been arctic. With the onset of winter, hot water-bottles were to be found hibernating in beds and a metal paraffin heater took up residence in the toilet. In those pre-permissive days, WCs were kept quite separate from ablutions and this one was more like a high-ceilinged corridor. The heater was an admirable attempt to bring comfort to exposed nether regions in the polar zone, but it gave off about as much warmth as the White Witch of Narnia. However, its vapours were intoxicatingly heady. The occupant was lulled into enough of a fume-filled reverie not to mind frostbite in embarrassing places.

My parents must have worked hard to preserve a certain style in the downstairs rooms; we sensed these were not activity playgrounds and largely played elsewhere. The dining-room had its elegant oval table and reproduction Chippendale chairs, a sideboard with delicate brass handles and glass decanters on display. One always gave particular fascination - a conical-shaped vodka bottle with a ballerina trapped inside, which some parent had gifted. Endlessly, I would wind up the musical box at its base and watch the tiny ballerina pirouette around her bell-jar in the sea of vodka, to the tinkling strains of Swan Lake. It was magical and probably sparked my life-long love of Tchaikovsky (and perhaps vodka).

Mostly we ate in the kitchen where steaming washing dried overhead on a wooden rack. The dining-room was kept for special occasions, such as Sunday lunch when we were allowed to choose our favourite bottle of pop to wash down the roast; or Sunday tea in winter when the fire would be lit and we would tuck into crumpets dripping in butter.

From time to time, our parents would have dinner parties from which we were tantalisingly excluded. There would be a flurry of preparation and dressing for dinner. I would stand in my pyjamas and watch Mum at her dressing-table, putting on her make-up like a starlet in her dressing-room. Mysterious pots of rouge and bowls of powder that left a scented dust behind. Mouth sculptured in crimson lipstick and then sealed by the pressing of ripe red lips on a handkerchief. Black hair brushed away from high forehead in waves. Earrings clipped on and perfume sprayed out of a bottle with a tassel.

There would be a hurried distraction about the ritual, as if the final curtain call had just been given. But not too distracted to notice a smut of soot or leftover crumb on a child's face. While temporarily off-guard, admiring the Cinderella transformation, out would come the handkerchief. Lick, lick, dab, dab. It was a peculiarly unpleasant way to be cleaned up, by a handkerchief smelling of lipstick and spit. Nothing to do but screw up the face and wait for the ordeal to be over - this evolutionary throw-back of a mother marking out her young with her smell.

(Years later, I caught myself doing it too - the quite involuntary movement of fingers to tongue at the sight of my children's faces still displaying items of breakfast. Lick, lick, dab, dab. Then a momentary pang of guilt as their sweet faces recoiled in disgust and forbearance).

As we grew older, we were allowed to stay up and meet the dinner guests and sometimes hand around nuts or the first course, before being despatched to bed. On these occasions, the dining-room would glint romantically in candlelight and the table would shimmer with glazed china plates, silverware and crystal, like a cave full of treasure.

Retreating upstairs, we would sneak onto the landing after goodnight kisses to listen to the chatter of china, the clink of laughter. We, like the proletariat of St Petersburg on the fringes of Tsarist conspicuous consumption, had a stomach-twisting feeling of missing out on the party. We didn't really know what we were missing and had a sneaking suspicion that we would have been bored into our soup if we had been there. But nevertheless, shivering by the banisters, it fed a nagging impatience to be able to do what grown-ups were doing - whatever that was. At the very least, dressing for dinner.

* * *

Across the hall, the sitting-room (or drawing-room as my parents called it) was a social place where people were entertained, school monitors knocked deferentially on the door and we played records on the gramophone or watched the black and white television. It was a civilised haven of glass-fronted bookcases, Encyclopaedia Britannica and Mum's writing desk that had belonged to her Victorian great-aunt, Amy Cameron of India Street in Edinburgh's New Town. A black carriage clock kept time on the mantelpiece; a gleaming brass coal scuttle stood on the hearth. The high-backed green sofa with eagle-claw feet had not yet been scratched to fluff by the cat.

Some mornings in term time, staff would come for coffee and stand around the elaborately carved Indian table that stood in the bay window. 1960s coffee was made with milk boiled in a pan and sweetened with sugar, but I was solely interested in the biscuits. I have pre-school memories of reaching past a curtain of black gowns in the single-minded pursuit of a Custard Cream or rich brown Bourbon.

Occasionally this oasis of civilisation was breached by a horde of miniature barbarians, we junior MacLeods. The attacks were governed by the seasons. Short winter days when the dark and boredom came early, when the fire was lit, were times of particular vulnerability. Black night beyond the curtains, leaping flames in the grate seemed to stir our mix of Celtic and Norse blood into primitive behaviour.

9

How else could my desire to set fire to things be explained? I really don't think I could blame the DIY children's programme, Blue Peter, for my inventiveness with burnt string. I discovered that if I took a length of thick twine, turned out the lights and dangled the end of the string in the fire until it caught alight, I had the makings of a spectacular Catherine Wheel.

I, plus a fraternal accomplice, would blow on the end of our homemade fireworks until they glowed red and then twirled them crazily over our heads like lassoes and cracked them like whips.

'Yee, ha!' we hollered, Lone Ranger-style, mesmerised by the dancing trails of red light we created in the dark. The fire would join in with an occasional fizz of blue flame, spitting out sparks of coal onto the hearth like a campfire cowboy.

If our parents were unaware of harbouring junior pyromaniacs, they knew about the sports fanatics. Long before cricket academies were popular, my brothers were advocates of indoor nets. Why they should choose to do so in the sitting-room and in front of the glass bookcase now escapes me. But eventually someone got bowled in spectacular fashion.

'Owzat!' The cry of being bowled was accompanied by the smashing of glass.

Rain of retribution stopped play. Sanctions were applied in the form of suspended pocket money and dire threats about boys and balls. Cricket under lights lost its appeal. Which may be why we took to indoor rugby. Or at least some loose form of the game which consisted of tackling each other to the floor by fair means or foul.

On one occasion my two eldest brothers, Donald and Torquil, were scrumming down on the carpet over a cushion. Thinking that it looked fun, Rory and I threw ourselves on top. We mauled and rolled and shouted in one heaving mass as Don struggled heroically to fall with the cushion over the try line (carpet edge). Just as he did so, Mum opened the door, no doubt alerted by the house shaking. The edge of the door and Don's cranium met in a headlong embrace. After the big bang, the stars were almost visible around his head. There was a second of silence.

Then the blood started. Noise, confusion, alarm. After sick hesitation, we ran upstairs after Mum who was steering Don into the bathroom. We peered from the door. Water was being run in the basin. Don bent over. We crept forward. Mum was too concerned with saving her firstborn's life to shoo us away. The water was ruby red.

'Is that all your blood?' we gasped in awe.

'Are you all right?'

'Does it hurt?'

What we mean is, will you die tonight?

Don was stoically saying nothing, or too dizzy to speak. Mum was calmly bathing his cut and saying something about the stupidity of fighting. But the admiration that we already felt for our eldest brother soared at the sight of his blood running into the basin and colouring the water. Later his forehead was bound in a huge white bandage like a half-turban by the house matron. We stared at him, this veteran from battle. He was separated from us by his exoticness, his bravery, his wounding by moving door. He was our hero for evermore.

Land Of Boy

The 'Boys' Side' was a warren of echoing corridors, bald carpetless floors and pale paint. Through the swing doors, sounds of life from this other world would waft to us - a shout, a slamming door, clatter of boot studs on concrete, a blast of music. It was a foreign land where the Boy species all dressed alike, slept in identical beds and roamed around in packs. It was a foreign land where the Boy species all dressed alike, slept in identical beds and roamed around in packs.

Blindfolded, it would have been possible to map your way there by smell. An exciting aroma of mud, jam, sweat and toast pervaded, along with a whiff of carbolic soap and pink cleaning gumption. The smell varied in subtlety and intensity depending on location. The prep hall was odour of ink and stale trousers, the studies more fragrance of marmalade and magazines with a hint of dead sock.

We made occasional daring forays into this mysterious world. At the top of the first corridor was the drying room, always warm as a muffin. We swung on the huge wooden racks and hid among the sails of clothing - pirates at sea in the tropical heat, leaping from ship to ship. We knew plenty of nautical banter from Dad, who used to rouse us from oversleeping in the holidays with the shrill of a bosun's whistle and some incomprehensible ditty about yardarms and eyeballs. No doubt it made perfect sense to the grog-fuelled sailor who first composed it, but it didn't translate well to children under ten. It went something like this: (Wail of whistle)

'Have o'! 'eave o'!
Lash up and stow!
Show leg, show leg!
Sun's up over the yardarm, burning your eyeballs out!
'Have o', eave o'!

(Followed by more ear-piercing whistle blowing). By then, we had usually got the message that hammock-time was over. Resentful as we sometimes were at this saltish behaviour, it equipped us for the language of the high seas.

'Hoist the main mast and pass over the yardarm!'
'Aye, captain!'
'Stow a leg in the topsail and pass the bosun's eyeballs!'
'Aye, aye, captain!'

* * *

The changing room was another area of fascination into which we would creep when the boys were out at lessons. It was an echoing chamber of baths and basins, lockers and duckboards, beyond which lay the inner sanctum of toilet cubicles. My sense of propriety kept me away from this holy of holies, until one day when I was exploring with a friend called Helen. She was the only black girl I knew. Helen, who was slightly older than me, lived down the hill and could giggle like a soda fountain. We heard someone come into the empty bathhouse.

A Boy! We both knew this by the drag of feet. With no way of escape, we clamped hands over mouths and scuttled into a cubicle. The steps got nearer. We hoisted ourselves up and clung to the walls like Spiderman so our feet could not be seen. Tall, leggy Helen was having problems. She needed her hands to stifle the explosion of laughter that was building up inside, as well as to keep herself off the ground. She was coming to the boil, small squeaks and snorts escaping out of her mouth and nose.

The boy went into another cubicle, did what he had to do with admirable speed and left. Maybe he paused to wonder if the cistern in the adjoining toilet was faulty or maybe he thought someone was in there with a particularly good edition of The Beano. But as far as we knew, he missed us falling off the walls in a burst of belly-laughing, light-headed at not being caught. Of course, Boy might have guessed we were there all the time. He probably went on to Hollywood and made a career out of suspense-filled toilet scenes. It's always struck me how many thrillers have a nail-biting moment in the gents where someone is holding themselves off the floor for dear life.

One trip to the changing rooms did not turn out so funny. Rory and I found a pair of weights lying on the bench. They were the old-fashioned round-balled dumb-bells that you see being lifted by moustachioed Edwardian strongmen in sepia prints.

'I bet I can lift them,' said six year-old Rory.

'Bet you can't,' said five year-old me, staring in awe at the double cannon balls.

He moved towards them, his small stocky frame tensing, his face under the red hair determined. Grabbing the weights he struggled and grunted. Then, defying science, they lifted. Only an inch or so off the bench, but they definitely lifted. A moment later he banged them down again with a triumphant smile.

It follows as night follows day and eyeballs follow yardarms that I must also try to lift them. If he could do it, so could I. With less than thirteen months between us, the world treated us like twins. Mrs Ward, our plump, cheerful and adored companion who came in to do some of the cooking, called us the Babes in the Wood. We were physically lumped together and mentally spliced. We were Robin Hood and Little John.

It looked easy. I reached for the weights. I strained and groaned. They might as well have been the Pyramids. Then unexpectedly there was movement. But it was not in the longed-for upward direction. In a flash they were rolling towards me like some cartoon missile in Tom and Jerry. Only time to gasp wide-mouthed like Tom before they crashed off the bench and landed on my foot.

I believe the scream of pain would have done a Disney cartoon proud. It certainly sent Rory tearing as fast as Jerry for help. I ended up in bed with a broken foot for a couple of weeks, which gave me ample time to reassess a career in weightlifting.

Nevertheless, I was determined to represent my country at something. Once time and bones had healed, I flirted with gymnastics. Trampolining to be more specific. Or to be totally accurate - bed bouncing. Well the house was full of them. I brought home two or three like-minded enthusiasts from school and we chose one of the boys' dormitories as our training gym. We bounced high, in circles, from one squeaky iron bed to another. Our enthusiasm and dedication would have brought a smile to the face of the most exacting Soviet Bloc coach. Surprisingly, it did not bring cries of appreciation from the boys who returned to find their regulation white sheets and woollen blankets in disarray.

Our hopes of getting to the Mexico Olympics came to an abrupt end with a knock on the kitchen door one tea time. Most mealtimes were interrupted by knocks on the door and round it a boy's head appearing with the words, 'Please Sir ...' This time it was the Head of House with a complaint about mysteriously ruffled blankets. Thumb screws were not needed - my red cheeks were an instant give-away.

Apologies were given and the lesson learned. It's stayed with me. The most successful present we ever bought our children was a large all-weather trampoline that occupied them outside for hours - and kept them (and their mother) from doing star jumps on the beds.

As for the dormitory beds on which I leapt, within a few years one of them would be occupied by my future husband. It's the sort of connection psychoanalysts could write theses about. But there was nothing Freudian about his teenage dorm experiences. Bouncing girls were but a distant imprint in the springs. Graeme remembers the lack of heating in the icy room being exacerbated by a friend, (a farmer's son and fresh air fanatic) who used to sleep with the window wide open in the middle of winter. Maybe Farmer Duncan was hoping for a whiff of clean Northumbrian air on the wind to remind him of home -or maybe it was to lessen the smell of mud, gumption and boy. Either way, his room-mates appear to have been too frozen to the metal bedsteads to get up and close the window.

* * *

Mostly, we waited until term ended before we explored the boarding house. Then we could safely play hide-and-seek in its deserted rooms and climb like mountaineers to the chilly heights of its dormitories. In term-time, we scampered from the glimpse of uniform, fled from footsteps and whistles, back through the swing doors to the safety of Our Side.

Christmas-tide: After the din of carol services and end-of-term plays, after the raucous singing of victorious rugby players coming to the front door and belting out, '*Floreat Dunelmia*' like de-mob happy veterans, after school trunks had been stirred from hibernation in dark cupboards and scraped along corridors to waiting cars - after all this -the house became ours.

In the school chapel, which high on its hill kept a benign watch over the school, a pair of Christmas trees twinkled either side of the altar. Once term finished, one of these large trees was brought like a trophy into our hallway and erected in an alcove. We would help Mum decorate it with gaudy balls (a few were new trendy and geometric), lights and tinsel. Our Gorrie grandparents and grand aunt Beth would arrive from Edinburgh to stay. Twice, the whole Gorrie clan came down from Scotland - two uncles, two aunts and five cousins taking over various dormitories - for a mass family Christmas. There would be catering and washing up on an industrial scale and a huge game of family football on the deserted school playing field.

Christmas Eve: the excitement would increase throughout the day, until the moment when Granny Sydney would sit by the fire sewing tape onto Dad's coarse, creamy-white sea-boot stockings for us to hang on the end of our beds. But before that, there was the trooping across Prebends Bridge, up the steep slope towards the Cathedral and through a dark, echoing tunnel to the Cathedral Close. Sitting fidgeting through the service of carols and lessons, echoing voices at lecterns trembling around the vast pillars. Light, candles, the crash of voices singing about Mary and Hark the Herald Angels and shepherds and Come All Ye Faithful - while all the time, the itchy thought excited that soon Granny would be sewing on the loops to the Christmas stockings.

By the time we emerge it would be dark outside, but still we couldn't go home yet. There was tea at the house of friends, a Canon of the Cathedral and his wife, Hugh and Constance Turner. Up the steps to their house in the Close, a large table set for tea and a smaller one by the fire for us, the youngest children. Miniature segregation. We sat on our small chairs and ate the treats they had kindly prepared, restless for the moment we could go home and let Granny get down to the serious business of sewing on the tapes. We wondered at the length of time it took grown-ups to eat tea - or stop laughing and talking long enough to eat it. Hurry up, *hurry up!*

Finally we would be clattering through the dark tunnel on our way home. Dad's socks were converted into Christmas stockings and hung on the ends of our beds. We were much too excited to fall asleep, but somehow we did. Waking on Christmas morning to the sight of a bulging seaman's stocking, the weight of it, the thrill of not knowing its contents greater than the knowing. Then we opened and compared.

There were more presents downstairs in the sitting-room - a chair per family member containing a small heap of gifts for each other - but we had to wait a lot longer for these. There were a series of obstacles, like the labours of Hercules that had to be overcome before we could open these presents.

For part of the holiday period, Dad was left in charge of keeping the ancient boiler going. This was no mean feat. The boiler was a greedy monster housed in a deep cellar at the back of the house and had to be fed gargantuan meals of coal at regular intervals. Hopping around in anticipation, we watched him in his boiler-suit flinging shovels of coal into the furnace, singing sea shanties like a stoker in a ship's engine-room.

'Hulla-ballu-balla-balay!'

It was mildly diverting, but would he please hurry up so we could open the presents. Of course, he now needed to clean up and wash his coal grimy face. Dad would go off for his cold bath (something he'd done every morning since his days on the Arctic Convoys to Russia in the War).

If we were lucky, we might get one present opened before it was time for chapel and the Christmas morning service. We trudged up the scores of steps to the school chapel (wearing new boots or jumpers if we'd been quick enough to open them) and sing once more about Mary and Hark the Herald Angels. Back at home the presents awaited, the games were unplayed, the chocolate Santas in their gaudy foil uneaten.

Finally, we were back out in the chilly air looking over the rooftops of the school to the Cathedral like a huge ship moored among the scaffolding of bare trees on the riverbanks. There was nothing now to stop us rushing home to open our gifts. Except Dad would be greeting some former pupils with laughter and an invitation to come back and have a glass of sherry.

So we hopped around in a frenzy of impatience, eyeing our presents while the grown-ups chattered and drank as if they had nothing better to do. And then suddenly, the moment would arrive when the impromptu guests were gone, the boiler was sated, parents and grandparents were rounded up and made to sit down and there were no more diversions between us and our Christmas presents. O Come All Ye patient brothers and rejoice.

* * *

Between the two distinct halves of the Caffinites lived the house matron and the house tutor. They inhabited a quasi-demilitarised buffer zone where both sides could visit. In the Sixties, out went tutor and music teacher, Peter Newman, with his tweed suit and well-polished shoes (who would later teach me piano) and in came hip tutor, Tim Stirk, with a flop of blond hair and his own TV (who would later choose me as his bridesmaid).

Betty Moore the matron, or Matey, as we affectionately called her, had a spartan bedroom and a more cosy sitting-room that was her home in term-time. She had a typewriter on which she patiently typed up my early attempts at story-telling and collected them in a folder. She was in charge of laundry and in winter I was drawn to the warm laundry room with its smell of starch. We would chat in cosy confidence about the boys (I usually had a crush on one of the older pupils) while we sorted the piles of stiff and gleaming underwear from creaking wicker baskets.

Apart from dispensing first aid to the boys she was useful in dealing with injuries among the MacLeod ranks, such as Don's split head. She also probably saved the life of one of my friends, Christine.

One Saturday when the boys were out at games, Rory and I, plus friends, were involved in a high-spirited game of 'chasey' around the corridors. Outside Dad's study there were swing doors that swung both ways that led into the boys common room and library. Someone ran through these with Christine following. She put out her hand as it swung back. Her hand went through a glass pane in the door. I arrived on the scene to find broken glass and blood. Somewhere ahead, Christine was being hurried upstairs to Matey's room. A trail of blood was on the orange and black stair carpet. There were shouts for help. Christine was silent, in shock, wrist cut. This was serious, for she disappeared to hospital.

Later, visiting her, a group of us from school gathered around her bed, giving her sweets. Quiet Christine, embarrassed by all the attention, was bandaged, a warrior from the chase. The swing door was re-glazed but ever after treated with fear and respect. Always in that memory were the splashes of blood on the jagged teeth of glass,
the fear. The scar on Christine's wrist was both a mark of her survival and an uncomfortable reminder that the accident happened in my house. I felt guilty by association.

* * *

There were times when Our Side was infiltrated by the Boys. Small waves of them would lap around the private doors to speak to the housemaster. As the '60s lengthened so did boys' hair and it appeared to be a source of perennial friction.

Dad would tell the shaggier members to get their hair cut or he would cut it for them. On occasion, he carried out the threat. Years later, he chuckled sheepishly at the memory of inflicting the kitchen scissors on one particular boy who was due to appear in an end of term concert. So radical was the transformation that the boy's own mother did not recognise him when she came to watch.

So the boys trooped in with their troubles or were summoned with the troublesome hair like petitioning subjects. Nowhere in our home was sacred. On at least one occasion, when time was pressing, Dad even conducted an interview with a monitor from the bath.

When we were small, to save time and energy, bath-times were mass communal affairs. Dad, several children, toy soldiers, sponges, cold cups of tea, boats and water sloshed equally between bath and floor. Into this steamy mayhem the monitor gingerly stepped. It must have looked like a scene from the last effete days of the Roman Empire. He cowered in the corner by the door while several pairs of eyes, peering over the rim of the bath, pinned him to the wall with their beady look.

I no longer remember why he felt it so urgent to talk to his housemaster, in fact I don't remember him saying anything at all - just nervous nodding and twitching. But it must have been a seminal moment in his development. He probably left the bathroom taking a vow of celibacy or, at the very least, determined to emigrate.

Some of the monitors we grew to like and were sorry to see leave. We had watched them win rugby trophies, screamed them on in swimming galas and applauded them in school plays dressed up fetchingly as women and directed by my mother. They were part of the Heroic Age of our childhood - larger than life, slightly remote members of a heroic pantheon which included The Beatles and our eldest brother.

I was destined for a quite different schooling and recall clearly that feeling of curiosity for the world beyond that gripped me at the age of four and a half. I grew impatient for the day, for I had lost my playmate. The day that Rory started school was filled with a terrible
dread. From the anxiety coming off my brother in waves, I was fairly sure I was never going to see him again. At least not for years, when he would be completely grown-up and have learnt everything. We walked either side of Mum, clasping her hands, down the back of Poole House and along the side of the allotments to St Margaret's Primary School.

The Juniors' was in a gothic stone building while the Infants' was housed in a low, dark wooden sprawling hut across the playground. We approached this brooding gingerbread schoolhouse like Hansel and Gretel. A bell clanged and the aimlessly running children swarmed like killer bees around the two entrances. It was time to prise Rory from Mum's hand.

We said our last goodbyes and watched him drag his feet like a condemned man, tears streaming down his face. I strained for a last sight of his bobble hat bobbing and waved and waved until my arm hurt. Then he was gone, swallowed up among the buzz of children.

'When will I see him again?' I asked Mum in distress, not convinced I ever would.

She squeezed my hand in sympathy. 'Lunchtime,' she said.

'*Lunchtime?*' I queried, incredulous.

'Yes, he'll be home for lunch,' she assured.

I felt a mixture of relief and anti-climax. Great, I was going to see him again before he grew hair on his face. But lunchtime! What had all the fuss been about? I wondered as we turned for home.

After that, the days dragged in a way they never had before. The nursery with its toys and smell of starched clothes airing over the fireguard seemed suddenly confining. Watch with Mother on TV and afternoon stories with Mum about tragic and heroic figures such as Roland and Hannibal were still enjoyable. But the imposed 'rest' in bed that followed was tedious. I spent it mostly out of bed, sitting behind the drawn curtains on the windowsill spying on the bustling world below and itching to be out there.

As winter came and my fifth birthday approached, my excitement at entering the world of School grew to bursting point. I had been led there like the proverbial horse to water, but not permitted to drink. Rory had told me about the kind Miss Allan and games in the playground. I'd even noticed that there were other girls in that playground to play with - a quite revolutionary concept. For up until now I had been one of the lads. Consumed by the desire to embrace this new world, I was blissfully unaware of how protected I had been from post-war patriarchal Britain. I had never been on the receiving end of sexual discrimination, simply because I had always been 'one of them' - an honorary boy. Now I was about to discover what it was really like to be a girl in a boy's world.

Casting Off

I was late for my first day at school in January 1963, which has more or less set the pattern for my time-keeping ever since. Dad had brought me down from grandparents in Edinburgh, where Mum was busy with another newly born rhesus positive baby. Yes! They had made it north of the border this time for baby number five. The whole process had been less than satisfactory. What seemed like ages before, Mum had confided in Rory and me one bedtime.

'I've got some exciting news for you!' she smiled.

'What? What!' we gasped. Father Christmas was coming early, perhaps, or Bill and Ben the Flowerpot Men were going to be on TV every afternoon.

'I'm going to have a baby,' she beamed. 'You'll have a new brother or sister.'

Silence. A baby. That appeared to be it; nothing else was forthcoming. Just a baby. Call me churlish. Call me Luddite about not wanting to give up my position as youngest in the squad, but I'd got more excited over episodes of *Andy Pandy.*

Rory mustered more enthusiasm. He wanted it to be a boy, so I immediately demanded a sister.

'When's it coming?' we asked, beginning to warm to the idea. Tonight? Tomorrow?

'Not for a few months - a baby takes time to grow inside Mummy's tummy.'

There was to be no instant delivery. The whole event was proving a huge anti-climax. So we carried on as before, with just the occasional reminder that there was another presence in our midst. One tea time, to our alarm, Mum lurched for the sink and was sick into it.

'The baby doesn't like peanut butter,' she explained, which made me question the sanity of our sibling-to-be.

As time went on, even one of Rory's schoolfriends commented on the expanding phenomenon that was Mum's tummy.

'You're looking a bit fat, Mrs MacLeod,' he observed.

Then we all decamped to Edinburgh for New Year and one day Mum was visited by a doctor and we were kept out of the bedroom. Next thing we knew she was gone to hospital to have the baby and excitement grew as in a betting office before the Grand National.

'Bet it's a boy,' my brothers taunted.

'Bet it's a girl,' I cried. 'I want a girl.' And I did. I had a creeping sense of a need for solidarity to counterbalance the overwhelming male hordes in some small way.

News came through that evening after I'd been put to bed. I was alerted by the cheers and splashing of my older brothers in the bathroom.

The news was confirmed, I had another brother. I buried my head in the pillow and burst into tears of disappointment. In time, I came to lavish sisterly love and bossiness on my infant brother, Angus, and would not have traded him in for anyone. But at that moment life seemed unjust and stacked against me. Mum was gone and, irritatingly, my brothers had been proved right.

School seemed an inviting consolation. So it was that Dad, dressed in his old seaman's duffel coat, took me into Miss Allan's classroom one January morning, late. The other kids looked up from their desks and stared at us, which may have given me a taste for the dramatic entry and a lifetime of unpunctuality. Miss Allan sat me at a desk with a lid and told me to look inside. There was a piece of card with some squiggles on it.

'That says your name,' she explained, 'Janet MacLeod.' I had to take her word for it. But it was a strange sensation, gazing at these lines that made no sense to me but conveyed meaning to those like Miss Allan who could break its code. It was the only strong memory I have of being illiterate and it was momentarily alarming, like being launched in water without a rubber ring. Apparently I returned home after the first day complaining that we had only worked in the morning.

'Then we just had *playing*!' I said in disgust. Well I wasn't going to crack the code by idling away the afternoon in the Wendy House.

In fact I never did get to play in the Wendy House because it was always too popular with other children - boys and girls. I can't have made a strong enough fuss over it, but I always had a secret hankering to know what on earth it was they all got up to in there. I have only ever been a semi-domesticated animal, housework being on the optional list of things to do. I blame this directly on not getting to play 'houses' in Miss Allan's class.

We loved Miss Allan. But halfway through the year, she changed into Mrs Burt which was very unsettling. We didn't trust this change; she was an Allan not a Burt and I couldn't help wondering if the transformation was really necessary. Why should she change her name? It was something to do with a Mr Burt, which seemed a tad selfish of him, interfering with the harmoniousness of the class. To our relief, she looked and acted much as before, but never again would she quite be the Miss Allan that we so trusted and loved.

There were other hard lessons to learn apart from literacy and name-altering teachers.

'Don't cry over spilt milk!'

This was how Mrs Burt chided me when I accidentally knocked over my break-time drink and burst into tears.

'Don't cry over spilt milk!' she said.

I was baffled. It seemed an eminently suitable reaction to having lost my favourite drink, soaked my clothes, flooded the floor and made a complete berk of myself in front of all the others. Why not over milk? Would spilt orange juice have been more deserving of tears? Life at five was full of such bewildering questions and adults often seemed a strange complicated breed.

But if I found that experience humiliating, at least I didn't have the bladder of a small boy. It never ceased to amaze me how often assembly would be disrupted by some boy wetting himself. We would gather in the hall - the large central room with two classrooms off either end in which the headmistress, Mrs Brown, had her desk. It was here that we were summoned to account for venial deeds and to be smacked with a ruler. My lack of imagination when it came to rule breaking meant that I only ever got smacked on the hand once - with that instrument of torture - the pencil.

The hall was also a happy space where we listened to the wireless and did Music and Movement. In pants and sandshoes, and in my element, I contorted creatively into a tree or a train or a rising sun.

But in assembly we would gather in neat rows attempting not to fidget and listen to Mrs Brown. They were not long drawn-out affairs, yet for some boys it was like trying to hold back the Aswan Dam. Usually it was during that moment of silence after the end of The Lord's Prayer when Nature would win over Nurture. The sound of pee cascading off bare knees and drumming softly onto the wooden floor would get our heads turning.

The mortified boy would be staring in stupefaction at what was happening beneath his shorts as if it had nothing to do with him. While he tried to convince the teacher that he was an innocent bystander, the rest of us would file out, thankful that for this time, we had been beyond splashing range.

* * *

On the home front, the genial Mrs Ward was still an important figure in the lives of Rory and I. We'd hover like flies in the kitchen while she made pastry or cakes, waiting for the moment we were allowed to lick the bowl. I would hinder her pastry-making by bringing out my miniature set of cutters and we'd make pastry men with the scraps.

For Christmas I got a set of toy pans which I think I used once. Into the largest I arranged a fistful of pastry, then lost interest and went off to play. Some weeks later, I came across the pans in the cupboard and to my horror and fascination discovered that pastry left to its own devices turned into something fit for the Sci-Fi series, Doctor Who; a furry green alien mass. With the steely efficiency of a time-traveller, I threw the whole lot - pan as well as primitive life-form - in the bin.

Occasionally, Rory and I went to stay at Mrs Ward's. She lived in a terraced house near the viaduct with a quiet, amiable man called Mr Ward. Together they provided an assortment of delights; grown-up daughters with trendy hairstyles, a twinkling-clinking cocktail cabinet in the corner of the sitting-room, a toilet in the backyard and a street full of children ready to play games, punctuated by the regular appearance of an ice-cream van.

The only dark cloud in this Eden was Mrs Ward's insistence that I still have an afternoon nap. What torture to be cooped up inside, wide-awake, when I could hear the shouts and laughter of the other kids playing in the street. Worse still, if the siren jingle of the ice-cream van floated in on a warm breeze.

With sustained pressure and Rory as advocate, my sentence was gradually reduced. I didn't have to stay upstairs, I could lie on the settee. From here I felt almost a part of the action going on through the open front door. The hour was cut to a half and then a quarter of an hour.

'Quarter of an hour!' Rory protested.

'That's only fifteen minutes,' Mrs Ward pointed out.

'Oh,' we answered, mollified. Fifteen minutes didn't sound half as long.

Eventually, I was given early release for good behaviour (or probably just annoying persistence) and the afternoon nap was abolished. This may have been the reason I was roaming at large one hot day.

The heat was bouncing off pavements and brick walls like a hard ball. I was alone (perhaps Rory was not here that visit) and had ventured to the end of the street, into Hawthorn Terrace and up the steep hill to where my new school friend, Joanne, lived. This was unmapped territory, out of sight of the Ward's house, where danger in the form of older boys lurked. I saw them out playing - bandits of the back lane - loud, restless and twice my size.

Returning home I was ambushed. A group of noisy boys (probably no more than eight years-old) shouted at me. I ignored them. They called and laughed. It was then I noticed they were armed. A silver pistol glinted in the air. I picked up speed down the hot hill, a Cherokee warrior pursued by cowboys. A boy taunted me, aimed the toy gun and fired. The crack of gunshot split the air. With a gasp I clutched my arm. I'd been shot! I could feel the pain.

Gulping for air and sobbing in fright, I sprinted back to the safety of Lawson Terrace.

'They shot me!' I wailed to Mrs Ward, falling into her plump bosom.

'Show me where it hurts,' she comforted.

I pulled up my sleeve searching for the bullet hole. I pointed to a miniscule blemish on my skin.

'There,' I said in triumph, 'and it really hurts.'

'They were probably firing caps,' she reassured.

I suspected the same, but could not admit it. I knew about caps. They were tiny dark rounds that came on strips of paper coiled in a box. You pressed them into the trigger of a toy gun and fired, causing a large bang and a smell like fireworks.

'Yes, but they can still hurt you,' I insisted, rubbing at my arm. The pain had inexplicably deserted me just when I needed it.

Mrs Ward colluded in saving face with sympathy and a drink of orange squash. But inwardly I was wounded by how easily the big boys had duped me. The deafening bang in the heat of high noon, my scream and clutching of the right arm - and then the pistol-whip of their laughter that chased me away. After that I stayed safe on home territory.

* * *

For a time I was friends with a manic small boy, whose name I have successfully erased from memory. It was a purely physical attraction - his mother was a fantastic cook. With the callousness of youth, I apparently returned home and told Mum, 'She cooks great food - better than you.'

The downside was the boy friend. When Toy Story was made, they modelled sadistic Sid on him, right down to the bit where he locks toys into his bedroom and terrorises them. Except my friend used to shut me in and refuse to let me go home.

Finally I resorted to the spilt milk method and burst into tears. When this made no impression, I cried louder and said I'd shout the house down. I don't know where his parents were all this time - maybe pinned to their bedroom wall with penknives - but they never seemed to intervene.

Eventually he tired of my lack of co-operation and opened the door.

'Go home then!' he screamed at me. 'Buzz off, you bizzy, buzzy bee!'

It wasn't quite the sinister language of Sid, but this was still the era of flower power.

It was this boy who first told me with glee that there was no such person as Father Christmas.

'He's not real. It's your parents, you know!'

I just didn't believe him. I left him as a poor deluded fool and shortly afterwards stopped playing with him altogether. In fact my interest in playing with boys at all was on the wane. I had new friends - Helen, Christine, Joanne and Jill at school, Bridget next door in Poole House and older Helen who lived down the hill - none of whom ever called me a bizzy, buzzy bee.

School was where we all learned sexual apartheid. In the Infants we still ran around with the boys and chased them as much as they chased us. But we could see how the world soon divided. In the Juniors the boys all played football on the far side of the playground near their outside toilets - an area into which girls did not venture. Junior girls played near the Infant school or in the middle of the yard. We played 'Tiggy on High' or mass games of skipping, taking it in turns to run and jump over a long rope held by two 'turners'.

'High, Low, Swing, Hop.'
'Jelly on the plate, jelly on the plate,
Wibble-wobble, wibble-wobble,
Jelly on the plate.'

Our games and chants were ritualised, passed down from nameless generations and picked up in the schoolyard, breathed in rather than consciously learned.

'Sausage in the pan, sausage in the pan.
Turn it over, turn it over,
Sausage in the pan. '

Then sometime in the mid '60s, the permissive society hit our Durham playground in the form of French skipping. All you needed was a long length of sheering elastic and at least two friends and this new obsession could be yours. The friends would be needed to anchor the elastic around their legs to form a rectangle and then the skipper would do complicated jumps and twangs in the elastic tramlines. The athletic labours would grow ever more Herculean as the elastic was raised like high jumps, from ankles to knees, knees to thighs, thighs to waists, waists to impossible dizzying armpit height. (Stunted friends were an advantage here). This was sexy skipping and we played it for hours.

If only one friend came home to play we would substitute a chair for one end, or a protesting baby brother. But neither was very satisfactory, being too short in leg and likely to move without warning. So the playground where legs, knees, thighs and armpits were plentiful, was the best place to play it.

* * *

By the time we were eight years-old, we went into an annexe classroom mysteriously set apart behind its own wall, between the Infants and the main Junior building. It was one of those temporary war-time Nissan huts that was freezing in winter and a wasp-infested hothouse in summer. Being there was like a rite of passage where we left behind the last vestiges of infancy and prepared for going into the upstairs classes in the Juniors where the teachers were all male. During that transition, boys became a nuisance or disgusting, or both. They picked their noses and ate their pickings. Michael Smith, knowing my phobia for things that wriggled, shoved a worm down my back, which might as well have been an anaconda for the fear and screams it provoked. About this time I had two ambitions, one to become an actress like my mother and the other to become a nun so I wouldn't have to marry a boy.

Presiding over the wandering tribe of eight year-olds was the no-nonsense Mrs Trotter and her 'pet' Jemima. Jemima was a dark seasoned leather strap that lurked menacingly in the top draw of Mrs Trotter's desk, coiled and ready to strike. Jemima was used against both the wasp population and us.

Jemima did not like naughty children, our teacher warned. If we annoyed Jemima, she would come out of her draw and strap the palms of our hands. It began to seem just a little bit more than coincidence that Jemima would inexplicably lose her patience at the same time as Mrs Trotter.

I no longer remember any of the misdemeanours that so riled them, but Jemima definitely had a preference for the taste of boy's sweaty palms. It was very rare, and so all the more shocking for a girl to be hauled out to the teacher's desk and strapped in front of the class. It never happened to me, though I can still recall the gut-wrenching fear I felt when a friend, Susan, was given the strap. But I am a coward, easily quelled by the threat of pain. As the great South African activist, Steve Biko, once said, *'The greatest weapon of the oppressor is the mind of the oppressed.'* My mind was certainly putty in the hands of Jemima.

The greatest punishment in the Junior School was to be sent to the headmaster, Mr Robson. This only seemed to happen to boys.

'Go and get me a sandshoe,' Mr Robson once said to a boy in my class, 'a big one.'

By the time the wretched boy had returned, I could almost smell the fear coming off him. He was taken into the headmaster's room and beaten on the backside with a size two. I was skulking outside ready to record some housepoints, but wishing I was upstairs doing anything else, even needlework, rather than witnessing my classmate's humiliation. Both he and the sandshoe survived, but I did wonder what it was about boys that so attracted the anger of teachers.

I didn't waste too much sympathy on them, for in other ways boys were getting a better deal. Once a week they were able to escape Jemima's gulag and disappear into the main building to do Art, while we girls were left to do Needlework. While I grew hot and sticky over a slippery needle and my piece of sewing turned grubby, the boys were splashing about with paint at the top of the school building like budding Wharhols.

My stitching was untidy and my knitting unpredictable. I sat there brooding over knitting needles like a French peasant at the foot of the guillotine, my knitting and resentment barely under control. The basic flaw in this craft was that I could knit but couldn't stop. I was the Sorcerer's Apprentice of knitting, incapable of casting off. This stood me in good stead as a teenager in the 70s, when long scarves were 'trendy'. I could have gone in the Guinness Book of Records for scarf knitting.

But it was absolutely no use to me in Needlework when the task was a petite knitted doll. Mindful of Jemima in the top draw, I did manage to finish the doll, although it took so long I never had time to sew on the woollen hair around its stitched-on plastic face. It was the first shaven-headed doll in the history of the school, a punk with one leg twice as long as the other, quite ahead of its time.

The generosity in my knitting was partly genetic. Mum, on the rare occasions when she took a break from mass catering or Alpine mounds of ironing, would sit down and occupy her hands with knitting. TV watching would be punctuated by the rhythmic click of needles and the cat would occasionally stir from in front of the fire to grab at an escaping ball of wool. It was a moment of excitement and honour to be chosen as the focus for the next jumper or pair of socks or cardigan, to suggest the colour and then watch it grow over the weeks.

And grow it did. Mum's home-made jumpers took on a life of their own. Like mother-love they were bountiful, all enveloping, expanding with wear.

One of Rory's grew into a mini dress which, worn over shorts, nearly had him arrested in the middle of Paris one summer holiday. As a teenager, I was devoted to a jumper of emerald green that doubled as a chastity garment, completely defeating groping boyfriends with its labyrinths of wool.

The last thing I ever knitted was a birthday waistcoat for a student boyfriend that I worried would be too small. It fitted with room to spare for his other three flatmates. After that, I laid down my needles for good, which is probably why Graeme decided it was safe to marry me. The waistcoat now languishes in our children's dressing-up box and comes out at Hallowe'en as something scary.

* * *

The whole of Mrs Trotter's class had weekly forays into the main building for poetry with white haired Mr Edwards. I enjoyed these sessions. We had a bond. At the time I believed it was because this teacher had spotted the poetic genius in me. But maybe Mr Edwards was just thankful that I didn't sit and pick my nose and flick bogies across the desks with rulers like the boys did.

I liked all my primary school teachers and we loved the students who came with their mounds of prepared material and asked us questions about ourselves. But I reacted strangely to having a male class teacher when we finally made it up the stairs into the lofty classrooms of the upper Juniors. Mr Welsh was new and young. He had replaced Mr Baron into whose soft stomach I had once run headlong one playtime. It had been a disorientating experience, running like the wind one moment, then stopped in my tracks the next and plunged into a dough-like darkness. I was rather in awe of stern Mr Baron, so surprised to find he had such a soft underbelly. I'm sure he had other reasons for leaving before I reached his class, but I think it was an intimacy neither of us wanted to repeat.

Mr Welsh had a shaggy fringe and a nice smile and improved my punctuality for at least a term. Yet inexplicably I was horrible to him. I planted a plastic spider pencil sharpener on his chair and in his jacket pocket. I showed off and answered back in class in a way I would not have dreamed of doing before. In short I was behaving like a boy, but had no idea why. Mr Welsh was just as baffled. Looking back, it was obvious I had a 'crush' on my first male teacher. I wanted his attention and didn't think I would get it by sitting passively and getting on with my work in the way girls were supposed to - the way I had always done up until now.

I thought he appreciated the witty banter, which showed how little I had grasped the rules of the game. For finally Mr Welsh lost patience. It was writing composition time. He was suggesting the topic - something riveting of the 'kitchen-sink' variety like 'A Day at School'.

'That's boring, Sir,' I said out loud and pulled a face.

He was suddenly thunderous. 'Just because all you can write about is hippies and fairies!' he snapped back. 'Well, some people find that boring.'

I was stunned. I thought he loved my stories. But he said 'hippies and fairies' with such disdain and in front of the whole class, that I couldn't think of one smart aleck remark in return. I flushed and bowed my head. It had meant to be a joke, but instead the laughter was on me. I was stung by his criticism. Maybe the odd groovy hippy did drop into my compositions, but this was late 1967, the year of Flower Power. The Beatles had gone psychedelic and Sandie Shaw was a puppet-on-a-string in bare feet.

After that, things were never quite the same again. We settled into a working relationship and there were no more confrontations. But neither were there any more hippies or fairies in my compositions, they had been banished by my suddenly self-doubting pen. At the end of the year, I asked Mum to buy a present for me to give Mr Welsh. It was writing paper or notelets with flowers on, if not fairies. I stood smiling self-consciously beside Mum as we said goodbye to him. He seemed pleased with the present.

'I thought at the beginning of the year, Janet didn't like me,' he told my mother in front of me.

How could he have possibly jumped to that conclusion? I wondered at his stupidity. Did he not realise that plastic spiders and cheeky remarks were a sign of adoration that I had lavished on no other? But I was now ten and suddenly tongue-tied and left Mum to say something diplomatic about my having enjoyed the year.

* * *

By the autumn I was in the top class and a responsible captain of St Aidan's house. The older Mr Dixon (with his Teddy-Boy haircut) was much keener on maths than composition and would have probably made short shrift of hippies. He was business-like and efficient, but not averse to a bit of leg-pulling and we worked hard for him as the prospect of the eleven-plus examination and Secondary School loomed.

The school cycle turned for the final time at St Margaret's. Winter came and break-time milk froze into hues of yellow and amber in the miniature bottles, then turned warm and sour in the crate come the summer. By that year, we had moved out of The Caffinites into a terraced house across the street and I took my youngest brother to school down Marjory Lane and waved him into the Infants'.

I was chosen by the school to go on Radio Durham and interview a university policeman, I'm not sure that either of us had a clue as to why. From the comfort of the recording studio we had to pretend that we were standing on the prestigious Palace Green, that divides Durham Cathedral from the Castle, and that I was lost. On the pretext of asking him for help, I then had to ask him searching questions about his job (something I had always been warned not to do of strange men). Far from arresting and incarcerating students, Bob's most exciting task appeared to be controlling the traffic flow and parking around the Green.

Maybe it was such nail-biting programming that made Radio Durham's existence so brief, despite being the journalistic training ground for the intrepid BBC reporter, Kate Adie. I've often wondered since, if I might have brushed past her in a studio corridor, rushing to my important interview on the front line with my uniformed informant, Bob. I like to think my piece of investigative journalism with that para-military of car parking might have inspired her to seek out the most dangerous assignments around the world's war zones. That way, my bizarre accosting of a university policeman on the pretext of being lost, would not have been in vain. I still have the bright orange badge to prove I was once there on the air. Its snappy Sixties logo reads, "I'm in the BBC Radio Durham VHF Set". I wonder if Kate still wears hers?

That summer term of '69 was filled with games of rounders in the schoolyard and trips to the town Baths for swimming. The tallest girl began to dress separately and word went round in whispered awe that her breasts were growing. We had conversations about periods and crossed our fingers that it wouldn't happen to us.

At the school Christmas party we had been allowed to wear 'stocking tights' instead of socks and felt very grown-up. One of the Helens began 'going out with' one of the Christophers and would hold hands on the way out of school. In the alleyway leading up to the school steps we would crowd around like courtiers at Versailles to ogle the royal couple and egg them on to kiss each other. If they did, the crowd would respond with a mixture of admiration and disgust.

'Ooh! Ugh! Eeeye!'

Slobbery boy lips and boy smell. It seemed far removed from the romantic love I felt for Sidney Poitier or some of the older boys at Durham School. Boys my age were just not hygienic enough to let nearer than arm's length. Which is where we kept them in country dancing class. When it was the girls' turn to ask the boys to dance, we revelled in our power to drag them protesting onto the floor. They feigned embarrassment, but were probably secretly relieved to be chosen. Little did I know it would be several years before I again got the chance to force a boy to dance or to sit amongst them in class. The days were numbered when I could turn round and tell the boys sitting behind me to shut up or we'd lose housepoints.

For with 1969 came the divisive test of the eleven-plus which fractured our friendships. This was the first year County Durham chose to assess the pupils' work rather than make us all sit an exam, but the outcome was still brutal. Those who passed went to the grammar schools and could be educated up to eighteen, the rest would go to the Secondary Modern, take lesser qualifications and be expected to leave at sixteen. Ours was also going to be the first year that they began to send girls to the boys' Johnston

School and boys to the Durham Girls' Grammar. We would be pioneers at the forefront of co-education, divided up between the old grammar schools not by sex but by proximity to the schools. Whereas those girls and boys who bore the stigma of eleven-plus failure, would be sent to Whinney Hill Secondary Modern and struggle against fulfilling their teachers' lack of expectation. They were like late-comers dashing for the grammar school 'train', only to be told that they had missed it and there would be no more down the line.

There were a few anomalies - a couple of girls whose parents paid for them to board a different train, to the private girls' High School, rather than knock around the station with the Secondary Moderns. Then there was me. I passed the eleven-plus, but by then it had been decided I would be going to a convent boarding school in Whitby. My parents were, as usual, treating me as the equal of my brothers and giving me the same opportunity to go to a fee -paying boarding school as they were having.

While the MacLeod boys were being sent north to Scotland in droves, I was going to Yorkshire. I told Mr Dixon this, expecting him to be pleased for me. But he obviously wasn't a regular reader of 'The Four Marys' (the boarding school heroines in my favourite comic Bunty) and knew nothing about midnight feasts and daring japes, for he looked dismayed.

'What do you want to go there for?' he asked in bafflement.

I didn't have a ready answer for this one. I just knew I would be pleasing my parents if I went. I smiled and shrugged. His look was pitying. Perhaps he knew something I didn't about convent schools, I thought with a tinge of foreboding.

'Won't you miss your friends?' he asked.

He had a point here. But Christine and Joanne were going to the Girls' Grammar, Jill and one of the Helens to the Johnston School. The other Helen and the other Christine were going to Whinney Hill. Susan was going to the High School.

'I'll make new friends,' I said brightly, trying to convince myself.

He shook his head and I was left with the feeling that I'd disappointed him, as if he'd been keeping a seat for me on the train and at the last minute I'd told him I wasn't coming. But I'd already sat the entrance exam and been offered a place at St. Hilda's in North Yorkshire long before the eleven-plus results came out.

Apart from Mr Dixon's ringing non-endorsement, the shine had been taken off my acceptance by the fact that my close friend, Helen, couldn't come with me. It would have made the whole prospect less daunting. I wanted her there and she was keen to come, all the more so since she had been sentenced to Whinney Hill, the Secondary Modern. For some inexplicable reason, the bright and sporty Helen had missed the 'train' and she had greeted the news by burying her head under her bed covers and weeping. St. Hilda's, we thought, was the solution. We could not understand what was standing in the way. Neither sets of parents seemed able to explain the subtleties of this educational apartheid to our satisfaction either. It was baffling and disappointing, but we accepted our parting of the ways with the fatalism of children.

The whole problem of who went where was traumatic for some and unsettling for all. There was an air of restlessness about those final days. For the first time in my school existence I began to feel bored. We had reached the top of the school - literally - we worked in the eaves and could go no further. I was ready for change.

We gathered in the playground for a class photograph on the spot where, years before, I'd fallen in a potato-and-spoon race and cried in frustration until Rory had come to comfort me. It was the place where we had done our cycle proficiency test and been awarded a *News of the World* 'Knights of the Road' badge and certificate.

We gazed out over the empty sloping yard which had grazed and pitted our knees with grit, where I had flown like a blue-bottle into Mr Baron's stomach. Over in the corner I had been knocked to the ground in my first term by a giant Junior retrieving his football.

'Sorry, titch!' he had called kindly. I had been incensed - not at being bowled over - but at being called a titch.

Behind us, leaves rustled against the high mesh fence and somewhere in the allotments lay the lost rounders ball I had hit high over the toilet walls. I had been awarded the rounder but declared out.

'Jelly on the plate, jelly on the plate, Wibble-
wobble, wibble-wobble,
Jelly on the plate ...'

At the final assembly - where we had so often played our recorders or fainted like felled trees as our growing bodies mutinied at having to stand still for long minutes - Mr Robson wished us well and handed each a leaving present. It was a Bible with photographs of the Holy Land. Clutching the shiny covers we left like pilgrims impatient for the journey ahead.

The whistle blew and we lined up in the yard for the last time, the calls of the playground echoed and stilled.
Don't cry over spilt milk!
Sorry titch!
MacLeod - you chase us!
Tig – you're on!

Then out of the gates we went carrying sandshoe bags and exercise books, filled with excitement at the summer holidays stretching ahead. We felt proud at having outgrown Primary School; we were veteran eleven year-olds, ready to take on the world - or at least down-town Durham. Nostalgia had not yet been invented for us. As we jostled and chattered and called out goodbyes, we left St Margaret's without a backward glance.

My Dad Was Ringo Starr

There was a joke going around my city when I was growing up. *Where does the Pink Panther live?* 'I don't know. Where does the Pink Panther live?' *Dur-hum, Dur-hum, Durham, Durham, Durham ...!* (sung to the tune of the Inspector Clouseau film, of course).

Maybe it was our way of putting Durham on the map, because we were proud of where we lived. The singer, Roger Whittaker, brought it a degree of fame with his languid ballad, 'Durham Town.' But it was obvious he'd never even been here, because we were a city not a town and we lived on the banks of the River Wear not the Tyne as he kept crooning to the rest of Britain.

For the benefit of Roger and those others unfortunate enough not to have visited, Durham is built on a series of steep hills and banks carved out by the twisting loop of the River Wear. In the middle it has created a peninsula - almost an island - on which tenth century monks took refuge from marauding Danes with the body of St Cuthbert. Above the river cliffs they built a Saxon church which was superseded by the magnificent Norman cathedral that still stands there today. Typical of the conquering Normans to take the attitude, 'Anything you can do I can do better.'

It may have taken forty years to build, with masons and craftsmen brought over from Normandy and a huge amount of labour for the building, but they did it. Not only that, but they revolutionised roof building with pointed arches and vaulted ceilings supported by flying buttresses. The Durham builders were at the cutting edge of Gothic architecture. It was a twelfth century Wonder of the World. And it must have done wonders for the local unemployment figures.

Scores of labourers were used in the quarrying and timber felling, clearing the wooded site and building scaffolding and sheds for the masons, let alone the towering abbey itself. They built massive pillars over seven feet thick and had to deal with modern masons just out of Gothic architecture school who wanted to build stone-vaulted roofs. Just imagine it.

'Listen lads, we've got this great idea! It's never been done before but...'

'What's wrong with timber?' the Durham workmen probably muttered amongst themselves.

But there it stands: an awe-inspiring, neck-cricking sight and testament to those medieval labourers. One wonders how grateful the Benedictine monks were.

'Well yes, it's beautiful, really beautiful. But did you say there's no heating? I mean all that stone ...'

'We've built you a warming house under the dormitories,' the architects no doubt pointed out, slightly peeved. 'You can have a fire on in there all winter. You'll be warm as toast.'

I bet the infirmary was full of monks with chilblains and bad circulation and haemorrhoids from sitting on stone benches in the Chapter House every day.

* * *

Across the Palace Green from the Cathedral stands Durham Castle, once palace to the Bishops of Durham and now a university college. Dropping away from them, the steep riverbanks remain heavily wooded. There's still an air of fortress mentality about the crowded peninsula with its monastic buildings - 'Half church, half castle 'gainst the Scot' as Sir Walter Scott put it - and its warren of medieval streets and houses jammed cheek by jowl as if preparing for siege.

For centuries, pilgrims have travelled to Durham to visit the tombs of St Cuthbert and St Bede, bringing valuable revenue to the community. And for us children too, all the most interesting sites were on the peninsula - like Woolworth's, for instance.

Going into the city centre was always an adventure. A trip to the shops entailed going 'Down Town' (as Petula Clark was singing in the '60s) and crossing over ancient Framwellgate Bridge.

My earliest memory, (more a sensation than a recollection) was of dipping backwards head first, the blank open sky above fringed with black - perhaps the hood of a large old-fashioned pram. I experienced vertigo in this world of hills and slopes long before finding my feet.

In the early days it was necessary to grasp a parental hand on steep cobbled South Street, then over the bridge and into narrow Silver Street, for wherever pedestrians could go, so could the motor car. The centre was semi-pedestrianised by the early 1980s, but before that it was a free-for-all. Traffic was supposedly controlled by a policeman in a box in the middle of the market square, but you stepped off the pavement at your peril. I know that because on my very first driving lesson in 1976, my brave and barmy instructor made me drive through the centre of Durham on a Saturday morning.

Maybe there were traffic lights operating that day, but I was in no state to notice. All I remember was the entire population of County Durham crammed into Silver Street for a morning's shopping, stepping nonchalantly from the pavement in the sunshine. They had no right to be so trusting, even if my instructor did have emergency brakes.

I wanted to shout out a warning. 'Please go home to your families. Stay indoors and keep your pets inside until further notice.'

Instead they parted like the Red Sea, while I prayed I didn't hit anyone I knew or who might be particularly friendly with my parents.

Afterwards, my instructor asked me darkly, 'Have you ever steered a car before?'

'Just the dodgems,' I replied, feeling light-headed we had all survived.

'I could have sworn you've steered a car before,' he said, looking relieved. Obviously I had swerved to good effect, but he never took me through the town centre on a Saturday morning ever again.

Back in the '60s though, trips downtown were especially spiced with excitement if we were going to buy some Beatles-related purchase, for my generation had been bitten by the Beatles bug by the time we started school.

Never mind screaming teenagers, there was a level of excitement on the steps of St Margaret's Infants' School back in 1964 that Ofsted School Inspectors would have died for. But we weren't discussing the latest Janet and John book - those moronic children in our reading scheme who could think of nothing better to do than help Daddy wash the car (John) or Mummy in the kitchen (Janet). No, we were picking up the scent of revolution on the breeze.

'Have you heard that new pop song?'

'Yeah! Which one?'

'She Loves You by the Beatles!'

'Yeah!'

'That's it! *She Loves You, Yeah, Yeah, Yeah!'*

* * *

Rory and I had been softened up for this experience. We had older brothers who already bought records. Torq was a big Cliff Richard and the Shadows fan and we knew the words to Summer Holiday as well as Cliff did. One night, the lights snapped on in the nursery where we both slept and Torq came in full of excitement.

'Do you want to see what I've got?' he asked.

Of course we did. Torq was our manager and mentor. He was good at supervising games and every so often he would organise us into putting on a play for the grown-ups which he would script, direct and act in. Usually they were about cowboys or knights and full of action. I once ruined a scene in a saloon by toddling unscripted up to the bar and demanding a drink, which must have been a bit scary to witness in a five year-old. So Torq was used to working with difficult actors.

But this particular night, Torq had something extra special to show us which was doubly exciting because we were supposed to be going to sleep.

'Yes, yes, show us!' we cried.

A moment later he was pushing a large board into the room. What was this? Stage scenery? He turned it round. It was a large pin-board covered in magazine pictures of Cliff and the Shadows. We were impressed at the display, envious that he had managed to collect so many pictures.

'What do you think?' he grinned.

We struggled to act unconcerned. 'Well it's quite good. But we don't like Cliff Richard. The Beatles are much better.'

'Yeah, we're going to collect ones of the Beatles!'

Torq gave us one of those looks that said he didn't understand the younger generation and dragged his board away up the corridor to his room. But he had given us the spur. We began to collect anything and everything we could about the Beatles. With pop pictures from comics like *Jackie* or *Fab 208* we did swaps with some of the boys in the boarding house. Like black-marketeers, we would sneak around the side of the house and knock on study windows.

'Pist! Want to do any swaps?'

'What you got?'

'Freddie and the Dreamers.'

'Get lost.' They were about to close the window again.

'Wait!' we cried like desperate Beatles junkies. 'We've got Cilia Black. Give you Cilia for that one of Paul McCartney.'

'Done. Now get lost.'

I would probably have swapped my tricycle and half my family for a photograph of Paul. He was my favourite Beatle and for a time I was helplessly obsessed by him. Rory, who was a John Lennon fan, once put me to the test.

'Who do you like best - Donald or Paul McCartney?'

I agonised, for our eldest brother, Don, was up there among the gods. 'Paul McCartney,' I finally decided.

'You like him better than our big brother!' Rory exclaimed with a mixture of awe and reproof.

'Well, I like them nearly the same,' I countered, feeling guilty, 'but Paul just a titchy bit better. I'd rather marry Paul.'

But it went deeper than that. For a time my identity with Paul was so great that I wanted to *be* Paul McCartney. I had the fringe and a tennis racquet as my guitar, so I could be a Beatle too. Once, staying at Granny's, I had such a vivid dream in which I was Paul that the next day I asked to go to bed early in the hopes of recapturing it. But it was a bit too early - the middle of the day in fact - and was so out of character that Mum thought I was sickening for something.

When I protested that I just wanted to go to bed and dream about the Beatles, this just confirmed my delirium and she called out the doctor. I wonder if I was the only six year-old who that bemused Edinburgh doctor ever treated for Beatlemania.

* * *

Back in Durham, we'd heard that Woolworth's was selling Beatle wigs. These would be just the finishing touch that we needed for our performances on the tennis racquets. We had to have them! Pocket money pennies were saved up and we waited with impatience for the next visit to Woolies. Rory, it turned out, couldn't wait. Hearing that a neighbour, one of Dad's colleagues, was going to Archibald's the ironmonger's, he applied his unique brand of charm mixed with annoying persistence until he was taken into town too.

But the plan went awry somewhere among the hammers and nails. The neighbour took so long in the ironmonger's, that Rory thought he would never have time to take him to Woolworth's, which lay tantalisingly across the bridge like Shangri-La. In annoyance, Rory gave up and stomped back up the hill alone.

The neighbour must have come out of his iron-filled trance to discover his small companion gone. The search and panic that followed ended in my brother being found at home and smacked for disappearing. So the moment when we finally got to buy our wigs should have been extra sweet. Sadly, those wigs were more magnificent in the anticipation than the wearing. For some reason I was gripped by the delusion they would be made out of something resembling hair. Mine would transform me into a Beatle look-alike.

To my dismay they were fashioned out of moulded plastic. The wig was a thin black plastic helmet. When worn for more than thirty seconds, they were sweaty and itchy and the sideburns dug in painfully to the cheekbones. Our reddish hair stuck out beneath these instruments of torture. We looked more like Ken Dodd's Diddy Men than Lennon and McCartney. But swallowing our initial disappointment, we strutted around the house believing ourselves the height of grooviness, suffering for our art.

Before we were old enough to venture down-town on our own and go straight to the record counter in Woolworth's (or later to Musicore, Durham's first real record store) shopping was an exquisite ordeal. There would be meat to be bought from Dewhurst's and bread from Carricks. We would be dragged into Greenwell's the delicatessen where each item had to be queued for at a separate counter. Assistants stood behind the long mahogany counters guarding dark wooden drawers of spices and shelves of tea and tins. It was always smelly - an exotic mix of cured meats and rich, spicy coffee beans - the kind of atmosphere that heritage museums now strive to recreate. But to the squeamish nostrils of a child it was a nose-pinching aroma of used socks rolled in sawdust with a hint of spam.

Afterwards, Woolworth's, with its sweet counter and shelves of gaudy treasures was an Aladdin's Cave of delights. But the biggest thrill of all was to ask for the latest Beatles single and pay over the specially saved pocket money or birthday token. Clutching the new purchase with more anxious care than a security guard would the crown jewels, that breathless walk back up South Street, along Pimlico and up The Caffinites' drive could not be over quick enough.

The first record I ever bought was, 'I Want to Hold Your Hand'. I still recall the feverish excitement of taking the black disc from its crisp, clean green Parlophone sleeve and placing it on the gramophone.

I'd swing the metal arm over to hold the single in place and move the play setting from 78 or Long Play to 45. Then the lever was pulled to release the disc. It dropped onto the turntable with a clunk and began to spin round, a dizzy whirl of thin black circles. The arm with the needle glided across and landed on its prey with a soft hiss.

A moment later, the first deep twangs of bass guitar boomed out in time to the thumping in my chest and the Beatles were released into the sitting-room. We'd be up on the furniture screaming, 'I want to hold your hand!'

Few experiences in life since have quite touched that peak of excitement felt on handling and playing that first single. A warm sitting-room bathed in sunshine, a sofa as stage, Rory as John, me as Paul. And a short blast of musical heaven that touches the soul that will be played again and again and again.

* * *

When the Beatles appeared on Jukebox Jury, the TV pop panel programme, it was a major event in the household. Only the screening of Winston Churchill's funeral had more of us gathered around the TV. (On that occasion, the TV had been wheeled into the large common room and I had sat squirming with boredom at the interminable processions and sombre commentary). As there was still no television in the Boys' Side, Dad allowed hordes of boarders to pack into our sitting-room for this national event.

Dad was more of a Gene Pitney-Dusty Springfield sort of man, but he obviously appreciated that this was a moment of deep cultural and educational significance. Jukebox Jury was one of our favourite programmes where David Jacobs compered a panel of celebrities who gave their verdict on new releases. Hit or a Miss. The fate of these pop hopefuls would be announced by Jacobs with the tring of a bell for a hit, or the rude blast of a buzzer for a miss. There was something gladiatorial about this programme, especially as sometimes the artiste was hiding behind the scenes without the panel knowing.

Even if the vote was a resounding miss, the hapless pop singer would have to emerge and meet the panel face to face, to the embarrassment of all. It was the forerunner of all those TV programmes whose addictive appeal is based on seeing someone else humiliated. It was Jerry Springer for kindergarten and we loved it, voicing our own opinions loudly at the screen.

I remember nothing of the programme's content the day the Beatles were on the panel, just that there they were sitting in front of us like real people. They weren't up on stage singing or playing guitars, but talking and joking in their exotic Liverpudlian drawl and flicking their fringes. It was high drama. This was probably as near as any fan would get to knowing our idols, I thought. That was until Rory and I had a mind-altering experience.

* * *

We were avid collectors of Beatles cards, small black and white photographs of our heroes jumping around in their matching suits in a variety of poses. The cards were carried around to amuse ourselves or stimulate conversation when adults were being particularly boring.

Among the eclectic group of grown-ups who were constantly turning up to the house to do boring grown-up things like drink tea and coffee and endlessly talk, was a venerable Victorian called Blackett. A Cambridge classics scholar and teacher, Blackett was ancient and bespectacled, dressed in black suit and gown. He was a link to a previous age and shaved with a cutthroat razor that his grand uncle had used at the Battle of Cape St Vincent alongside Nelson in 1797. He would travel into Newcastle to have it sharpened and was very upset when eventually told that the eighteenth century blade was too thin to sharpen.

'It's worked perfectly well since Cape St Vincent,' he blustered, obviously aggrieved at the parlous state of modern British craftsmanship.

To add to his bewilderment, Rory pranced up to him one day waving Beatles cards under his patrician nose.

'Would you like to look at these, Mr Blackett?' Rory asked, ever an optimist.

To my surprise (for I was much in awe of black flowing robes and talk of naval battles) the old scholar took the photographs and scrutinised them. It was no cursory flick through the precious collection; Blackett studied them. Maybe he was a secret admirer of our favourite band? I thought in mounting excitement.

Finally he looked up. He pointed to one of the cavorting black suited figures.

'Is that your father?' he asked Rory.

We stared at the picture in astonishment. He was pointing at Ringo Starr. We stared back at Blackett. Was he mad or as visually impaired as Horatio Nelson? What would our dad be doing jumping around with The Beatles in a tight black suit and Chelsea boots? Besides, Ringo Starr didn't look anything like our dad.

It really did beg the question as to what the ancient teacher thought Rory had been showing him. Staff photographs? VE Day celebrations with fellow matelots? It was baffling and confirmed my suspicion that grown-ups could be really quite dim at times.

The dim-wittedness of Cambridge scholars did not dampen Rory's enthusiasm for showing off his cards. Nobody, no matter how old, was exempt. Granny MacLeod, Dad's mother, was one of the oldest people we knew and by the early 1960s was in her late eighties. Brought up in Victorian Edinburgh with a twin sister and brothers, the daughter of a Bank of Scotland inspector, Mary Campbell Faill had lived through umpteen social upheavals. She had seen the bustle give way to the bathing suit, the horse carriage to the motor car. She had lived through the fall of Tsars and Kaisers and the rise of flappers' hemlines.

Artistic and an accomplished golfer, Mary had married her childhood playmate and brother's schoolfriend, Norman MacLeod in 1906. The son of Donald MacLeod, a charismatic Church of Scotland minister, who preached to Queen Victoria at Balmoral and ministered to Scots in London, Norman was sent back to Scotland for schooling. As children in Edinburgh, the genial and exuberant Norman would write plays in which Mary would always be the heroine and he the villain. Later, as a divinity student in St Andrews he was President of the Shakespearean Society and cut a dash around the town dressed in sweeping gown and top hat, entertaining his fellow students to imitations of Sir Henry Irving whom he had seen perform in London.

Ten years later, the patient Mary married her sweetheart, now a minister himself and took on the role of wife of the manse. Like most MacLeods, he can't have been easy to live with. An idealist, who angered his father by refusing to take on a safe parish and a secure living, he rushed off to Glasgow to work in a mission in poverty-struck Tradeston. Finally he took charge of a church in Lossiemouth on Scotland's north-east coast, serving the poor fishing community. But it had no manse to offer a wife and he lived in digs until something (maybe divine intervention) prompted Norman to propose to Mary and rent a house.

Eight years on, they moved down the coast to Belhaven in rural East Lothian and a manse of their own, which Norman proceeded to fill with as many visitors as possible. MacLeods like nothing better than to pack a house full of people and leave the logistics of feeding and entertainment to someone else, usually the long-suffering spouse. The parable about the man who searches the highways and byways for guests to drag home and feed is a fairly accurate portrayal of a routine day in a MacLeod household. Liberal in outlook, Norman was just as likely to invite the Roman Catholic priest from Dunbar, with whom he was great friends, as he would members of his Presbyterian flock.

Mary, when not bridging or golfing, played the part of Martha and coped with the invasions. Yet revolt must have been simmering. As a middle-aged woman, she shocked her family by cutting off her long coils of hair and having it bobbed, which must have been one of the most revolutionary acts ever witnessed in their quiet country parish since the introduction of the seed drill.

Mary had already refused to emigrate to Canada where Norman had been offered a prestigious Toronto church, for her protective father and twin sister could not bear her to go so far away. She knew what she was turning down, for they had spent a month there, travelling out on a liner just after the Titanic went down. It was comfort and wealth far beyond what Scotland could offer; a new life for daughter Molly and a fresh start after a botched birth and painful stillbirth of their second daughter.

But family pressure prevailed and they stayed. Which is why my father (who came as a complete surprise to a couple in their late forties) was born a Scot and not a Canadian. Molly remarked in later years that her adored father felt rather usurped by wee Norman's arrival. Certainly, Mary and Molly lavished this latecomer with boisterous love and fussing attention, as did the wider family. One of the Irish Roberts cousins who enjoyed hospitality at the Belhaven manse in the early '20s, brought Dad some toy soldiers but he preferred a more spiritual flavour to his games. 'You were a dear wee boy,' she reminisced in a letter, 'so busy with the burial of your pets and I would act as chief mourner and it was great fun.'

Neither was wee Norman in any hurry to begin formal education. At the age of five, Auntie Molly walked her small brother the two miles into Dunbar to start school. She walked back feeling bereft, but no sooner had she arrived home than a car drew up outside the manse. Young Norman was sitting in the passenger seat, bold as brass. Deciding he did not like school, he had persuaded someone to run him home.

The older Norman could be stubborn too. Maybe it was to get his own back for Toronto, or his young rival, or maybe the manse felt suddenly empty with Molly away at university. But about the time my grandmother was cutting off her hair, her restless husband accepted the bustling parish of St Bride's in Partick, Glasgow.

Apart from being dragged into the teaming city, the main drawback was that the position came with no salary; the minister before him had had a 'private income.' Not one to ever worry about money, Norman threw himself into his busy parish, building up a reputation for giving a good service and being especially effective in comforting the bereaved. He was highly popular and liberal in approach, as well as being an authority on Church Worship.

His young son remembers him as full of fun, a practical joker with his schoolfriends. My father seized on these moments of attention. Yet he did not thrive in Glasgow and was eventually sent to boarding school in the Perthshire countryside 'for his health' where at last he began to enjoy life. Meanwhile back home, the hospitality (and convivial drinking) continued and the money (Mary's) dwindled. Molly got married and moved to Edinburgh. Beneath the veneer of a welcoming manse, the marriage must have been crumbling under the weight of financial strain, past disappointments and generous but profligate MacLeod behaviour. Young Norman came home one holiday and remembers his father taking him to the pictures. He was sixteen.

'Would you like a cigarette?' his father offered him, man to man.

'No thanks,' said my dad nonchalantly, 'I smoke a pipe.' As he produced it, the older Norman roared with laughter. Here was a son he could identify with; someone whose company he could begin to enjoy on a more equal footing. My dad went back to school. He never saw his father again. For by the next holiday his parents had separated. Mary, whether pressurised by her family or not, had had enough and moved back to Edinburgh.

'In those days,' my Auntie Molly recalled painfully years later, 'you had to take sides.' Although her father maintained contact of sorts, via Molly's lawyer husband, she did not see her father again either.

The Second World War came as a diversion from the traumatic family rift and Dad soon joined the Navy as a nineteen year-old seaman. His first ship, The Glengyle, docked at Greenock and one night he decided to go ashore for a pint before closing time. He returned to discover a man had been to the ship asking for him. His father.

Young Norman's initial reaction was relief that he had missed him. He was embarrassed to think of it. What would he have said to this man who had caused so much upset to his mother? What would his mates have thought of him? He wasn't supposed to see him. It would have felt disloyal to his mother, to his aunt.

But later, at sea with time to reflect, Dad was left with the burden of regret, of an opportunity missed. His father had followed his movements from afar, known of his joining up. He had sought him out when his ship was in port; he had wanted to see him again. He was not rejected. So young Norman wrote to his father. His father wrote back. There must have been a reconciliation of sorts - a healing of raw wounds. Yet the fledgling correspondence was short-lived. In January 1942 (while young Norman was on the convoys to Malta), during the harsh snow-storms of that bitterly cold winter, his father died. The vast church of St Bride's was packed for his funeral, but the severe weather denied him his final wish to be buried in Lossiemouth (that place of youthful idealism among the fisherfolk, of early happy marriage and the birthplace of his beloved daughter). Trains north were completely snowbound, the earth was too hard for burial. Rev. Norman MacLeod was interred in the vast Western Cemetery in Glasgow. His obituary recalls his courage and genial personality as well as his keen and active mind. "A true Christian, he had little patience with sectarian differences ... none sought his advice and help in vain. He will be remembered best as a true son of consolation."

By the time we knew Granny MacLeod, her rebellious hair was quite white and the lithe body that had once acted the girlish heroine and swung golf clubs was virtually bed-bound. When she was still able to travel, she would set up residence in the spare bedroom where she would receive us children after breakfast in bed. Breakfast on a tray, on a special table was one of the exotic rituals that surrounded Granny. The other was a startling piece of furniture that looked at first like a rather grand chair. But the seat lifted up to reveal a porcelain basin inside. Some secret storage chamber? I pondered. Perhaps for Granny's toffees?

'What's this for?' I asked Mum, intrigued, as she made the room ready for Granny's arrival.

'It's a commode,' she explained. Or rather didn't.

'What's a commode?' was my obvious next question.

'It's for spending a penny. It's easier for her than getting to the bathroom.'

I was electrified. What a brilliant invention. Why didn't we all have one? It was so much more prestigious than the pink and white tin potty I had under my bed in case of emergency at night. I opened and closed the lid several times in appreciation before Mum bustled me out of the inner sanctum.

So we looked forward in excitement and a little trepidation to being allowed in to see Granny in the not-too-early mornings. There she sat with a dark red shawl around her shoulders, propped up by a mountain of pillows and cushions like a tribal queen giving audience to her small subjects, her throne-like commode in the corner. She looked incredibly old and wise, her straight regal nose rather severe, her skin stretched like ancient parchment across her cheekbones.

Then her face would soften in a welcoming smile and she would beckon us forward with a raised hand and a deliciously Scottish voice. There was an unwritten contract between us children and our oldest grandparent, who had outlived her estranged husband by over twenty years. We knew that if we sat on her bed and talked for a bit, we would be rewarded with a square of toffee. There was nothing quite so succulent or decadent as a mid-morning Granny's toffee. We delighted in the crackling of the cellophane paper as we unwound the twisted ends, the crinkled look of the tawny sweet in its hardened state, like ancient bedrock. Then the first nectar taste as we sucked in concentration, transforming the toffee to its molten state until it was soft enough to chew. Finally came the contented aftermath of sticky fingers trying to gouge the last remnants from our back teeth, the tongue sated in sugar.

We knew nothing of the sadness stored up in Granny's ninety year-old life. We did not ponder why she should so fuss over our baby brother. Her delight in babies was baffling. But the joys of toffee eating we could share.

When travelling to Durham was another enjoyment curtailed by creeping old age, we would go to visit Granny in her Edinburgh nursing home. Dark wood, patterned carpet and the strangely comforting smell of incontinence were what struck me as we mounted the large staircase up to her bedroom. I would take my new red drum with the stretched rubber top to play to her. My rather expert drumming, I liked to believe was the highlight of these visits for Granny.

Rory, however, believed nothing could compare to his Beatles cards.

'Granny, would you like to look at these?' he asked, bursting with pride as he handed them over. And just to make sure there was no confusion this time, he added, 'They're The Beatles.'

He moved restlessly from one foot to the other as she took them in shaking hands and gazed at the young men in the photographs.

She pointed to one and looked up at our expectant faces.

'Is that your father?' she asked with interest.

Rory's face briefly showed disappointment. 'No, Granny,' he sighed, trying to mask his impatience with the older generation. 'It's Ringo Starr.'

I looked with incredulity from my father to my drum and back to my father. It's true that my dad could play the drums. He regularly borrowed mine and paced the floor at night with baby Angus, thumping out a tune. It was the only method of getting my restless baby brother to calm down and go to sleep. (This went on for two years and caused my parents serious sleep deprivation, while Angus grew up to have fantastic rhythm).

But this was quite incredible - fab really - that my father could be mistaken for one of the Beatles, not once but twice, and by his own mother. There should have been a drum roll. Because for one brief heady moment - at least in the minds of Granny MacLeod and me - my Dad was Ringo Starr.

'I Want Never Gets'

Certain phrases used to crop up almost daily in childhood. 'I want never gets', adults would say, prompting us for the umpteenth time to remember to say please. Or the one that used to fill me with frustration; 'Your turn will come.'

Usually it was spouted forth when the elder brothers were allowed to do something we younger ones were not. Stay over at a friend's. Go to a party where they danced to Cream instead of eating it with jelly. Watch scary *Adam Adamant* on TV or be taken to see Omar Sharif in *Dr Zhivago.*

'Your turn will come,' Mum would try and mollify our impatient cries of protest. But we knew it wouldn't, or certainly not nearly soon enough to satisfy the craving of the moment.

That is why it is truly frightening to hear these phrases still persisting into modern day. Worst of all is how these sayings now trip off my own tongue. Having lain dormant for decades, they pop, unbidden from my mouth to infuriate my own children. It's as if a time capsule has been buried deep within that someone has maliciously opened. A Pandora's Box of homely wisdoms.

There was nothing that accentuated the Generation Gap more, in the 1960s, than the watching of Top of the Pops. It was a Thursday ritual that we would not miss for anything. My parents tolerated it, despite their alarm at my adulation of the hedonistic pouting Mick Jagger. The clean-cut Beatles in their smart suits they could handle. The Rolling Stones, strutting in their polo-necks and shaggy hair, were far more subversive. One of the first singles I ever bought, was Mick Jagger's raunchy It's All Over Now, little guessing how it was giving my parents sleepless nights.

'Is that a girl or a boy?' Dad would ask teasingly, causing us to groan, fall off our seats and roll eyes heavenwards.

Mum, the professional actress with perfect diction, would add for good measure, 'I can't understand a word they're singing.' Half the time, neither could I, but her criticism was hardly in the spirit of pop.

Staying with grandparents, Thursday evenings were always tinged with nervous anticipation. Would we be allowed to watch *Top of the Pops*? We would be extra polite at the supper table, squirming in our seats as we waited to be allowed to escape adult company and watch our favourite programme.

The grown-ups had the most astonishing capacity for talking, often politics or the international scene, as the grandparents had worked in India for many years and still rushed off to conferences and lecture tours. Granddad was a forester and a world authority on soil erosion and Granny a member of the Women's Council. Dad's politics were stuck in the nineteenth century. 'I vote for Disraeli!' he consistently declared and therefore voted Conservative no matter how badly they behaved. Ironically, in 1945, after five years of being an ordinary seaman and reading the liberal Manchester Guardian sent airmail by his Auntie Bessie, he was poised to vote Labour. But his mother filled in his proxy vote in favour of the Conservatives.

Granddad, I believe, had lurking Scottish Nationalist tendencies, as he was a great admirer of their star MP, Winnie Ewing. It was from one of his pamphlets, called *Black and White* that I first learned of the discriminatory laws of South African Apartheid. Auntie Beth, Granddad's only remaining sister, who was often around for meals when we visited, had been a young activist for the Pankhursts in the fight for British women to win the vote.

Mum, when finally released from the burden of childcare, went into local politics and became a Liberal councillor for both Durham City and the County Council. Her youngest brother, my Uncle Donald, went further still. He was to serve as a Liberal Democrat MP for Edinburgh West and after Scotland secured its own Parliament again, he became one of its radical campaigning MSPs. But this was all in the future and we sat at table unaware that we were part of this crucible of political ideas. We cared only for the melting-pot of pop.

'Thank you for supper, Granny. Please may we get down, Granny?'

'Yes, dearie.'

'Please can we watch Top of the Pops, Granny?' We would hold our breath. No good asking Granddad, because his disapproval went far beyond Mick Jagger's swagger. He couldn't even stand The Beatles.

'Yes, dearie,' Granny would grant permission, with a twinkle of blue eyes behind glasses and a gauze of cigarette smoke.

We rushed for the sitting-room and gathered on the carpet beneath the TV which was perched high on top of a cabinet, as if by putting it so far out of view it would do us less harm. It just meant that by the end we had cricks in our necks. Torq, who was tall enough to reach the buttons, switched on the TV and put on his glasses, the better to appreciate Pan's People - those blonde, grinning, rubber-legged dancers.

Sometimes, unsettlingly, Granddad would come along too. Not to watch, but to sit on the far sofa and read the newspaper noisily. The hit parade was punctuated by Granddad's harrumphing and shaking of his paper in disapproval. Only when Pan's People appeared did the newspaper drop its guard for any length of time.

This scene must have been enacted in countless homes across the country every Thursday evening at half past seven. For in a house in Wallsend on Tyneside, my husband was going through the same ordeal with his grandmother.

'Is that a girl or a boy?' his Nana would ask, shaking her head in incomprehension that such beautiful long hair should be wasted on a man. 'And what's he singing? I can't understand a word.'

A generation on, we were plaguing our own children by insisting on watching TOTP with them (by this time rescheduled to a Friday night).

'Why are they wearing those thick coats?' I would find myself commenting on the over-dressed performers.

'It's cool, Mum,' they'd say.

'Looks boiling to me.' My answer would cause them to fall off their seats, groaning and rolling their eyes heavenwards.

And when the children cheered enthusiastically for a song they liked, we would say infuriatingly, 'This isn't new, you know. We were dancing to this in the '70s.'

Then the day came. 'Is that a girl or a boy?' Graeme asked. He had finally turned into his nana. Scary.

* * *

Our TV watching was often directly linked to the games we played around the house. If we were very good, we were allowed to stay up and watch The Man From U.N.C.L.E. after Top of the Pops. The two male agents were the role models for my friend Helen and me - she the enigmatic Russian blond Illya Kuryakin, I the suave dark-haired Napoleon Solo. We rushed about feeling cool-headed and slinky in our nylon Marks & Spencer slacks with stirrups under our shoes, Helen talking into her dad's Remington shaver.

The cavernous boarding house held a warren of hiding places, best of which was a creepy dog-leg passage known as The Slides (accessed by sliding doors) where school trunks and luggage were stored alongside cleaning materials. The Slides were dark and smelt of carbolic soap and polish. When Angus became old enough to play with us, we would enlist him as the baddy. On one occasion, heartlessly, we left him behind in The Slides. On another we dressed him up as a Dutch girl and couldn't understand why he made such a fuss. (Actually, forty years on, he's still making a fuss about it).

I loved to dress up. After watching The Lone Ranger, Rory would become the cowboy, while I was the 'Indian', Tonto. For extra effect, I would rummage in the bottom of Dad's wardrobe for liquid shoe polish and smear warrior streaks of medium tan across my cheeks and chin. In every Western, I would cheer on the 'Indians', for they were handsome and brave and made a wonderful whooping noise, and it was always a mystery to me why they never won any battles.

I was used to playing the supporting role in games with Rory, for somehow he always seemed to get to play the star part.

'I'll be Robin Hood, you be Little John,' he would suggest as if doing me a huge honour. I went along with this, because Mum had once acted with the TV Little John and so there was glamour attached to the role. But when we came to re-enact the fight with sticks (cricket stumps) on the log over the river (cricket bat on rug), Rory would remind me.

'You end up in the water, remember.' Ugh, splash! I made the moment as dramatic as possible and rolled around on the nursery carpet.

'Now you be one of the Sheriff of Nottingham's guards,' Rory ordered. I leapt up and grabbed a plastic sword. Despite my deft sword play, Robin Hood had soon knocked me over the castle ramparts. I became another soldier. Two minutes later, I was dead again. This time I put on the plastic breastplate, helmet with visor and battered plastic shield.

'I'm the Captain of the Guard!' I cried in a muffled but triumphant voice from behind the visor, thinking myself invincible this time. But soon there was a siege and a fight to the death with the men of Sherwood Forest. Robin fatally wounded the Captain, but I took several minutes of agonised groaning and writhing on the floor before succumbing to death. By this time, Robin was already hopping it back to the leafy forest for the celebrations.

There was only one thing for it. I rushed off to the dressing up box in the linen cupboard and found a cloak. Returning to the nursery, I announced with a flourish, 'I'm the Sheriff of Nottingham! I don't die; I'm on the telly every week!'

Play acting William Tell, called for even more leaps of imagination. While Rory inevitably was the crossbow-wielding hero, Tell, I was usually a short-lived soldier. On occasion I even had to resort to being the fat and unattractive baddy, Gessler (played on TV by Willerby Goddard, another star that Mum briefly acted alongside).

For countless games I never questioned Rory's right to take the hero's role. He was older than me and more worldly wise; it was his due. That was until one fateful night - one of those defining moments when a small girl's world paradigm alters for good - and caused my acting career to change direction.

I was snuggled cosily in bed in the chilly nursery, drifting off into beckoning sleep when Rory's voice came out of the dark.

'Jan? Jan! Are you asleep?'

'No,' I admitted from beneath my warm covers.

'I can't get to sleep,' Rory said, tossing and turning noisily. I peeped out from my warm nest and peered through the dark. It looked as if a volcanic eruption had taken place in the bed opposite. There were blankets and sheets strewn crazily over the bed and spilling onto the floor. Somewhere amid the boiling mass of material was a hot and bothered brother.

'I know!' Rory's voice emerged again from the chaotic heap that was once a bed.

'What?' I asked sleepily.

'Let's play Florence Nightingale!' he suggested. I respond to the word 'play' and lift my head off the pillow. 'You can be Florence Nightingale,' Rory said magnanimously, 'and I'll be a wounded soldier.'

'You mean I can be the main part?' I asked, just to be sure.

'Yes. You be Florence and come and tuck me up in bed,' Rory assured.

This clinched it. I was to be the star.

I climbed out of my warm bed and set about playing my part. Busily I rushed about untangling sheets and pulling blankets back on the bed, tucking the ends carefully into 'hospital corners', while Rory lay immobile as the wounded soldier. It took ages. After some time, I became aware of how cold it was in the dark bedroom, of how cold *I was*.

Rory had his eyes closed on the newly plumped pillow. I did a final tuck round and then clambered back into my bed. It was freezing. So was I. I was also fully awake. I lay there trying to warm up.

'Rory? Rory! Are you awake?' I hissed. There was a gentle contented breathing coming from the peaceful bed next door. He was sound asleep.

I lay for ages, cross, cold, sleepless and indignant. This had nothing to do with playing the heroine. I had been spectacularly duped into re-making my brother's bed. And now he was asleep and I wasn't.

After that it was never quite the same. Terms of contracts had to be negotiated up front. The Captain of the Guard could become quite uppity, insisting that he was not killed off - at least not in the first episode. And never again did I play Florence Nightingale. Female parts were boring and sissy - apart from Cat Woman who was twice as smart as Batman and wouldn't have been seen dead making hospital corners for anyone.

* * *

It was such incidents as the Florence Nightingale con that fed my nascent feminism. My first inkling that all was not fair between the genders was being thwarted of my first career choice to be a sailor. As a five year-old, I used to love dressing up in one of Dad's old sailor hats in preparation for when I grew up and went to sea. Then one day, after sailing the high seas in the drying room, I learnt the brutal truth; 'Girls can't be sailors'. It seemed incomprehensible.

'Why?'

No one could explain, not even Mum. 'Only men are sailors,' she said lamely, 'but women can be WRENs. You could be one of those,' she tried to console.

A WREN did not have the same swashbuckling sound to it as Jolly Jack Tar.

'What do WRENs do?' I asked, dubious.

Mum didn't seem too sure. 'They work onshore doing paperwork and things.'

'Not on ships?'

'No, they don't go to sea,' she admitted.

What, I wondered, was the point of that? I gave up my naval ambitions in disgust and looked on boys with envy that the world was their oyster.

So, lacking female role models apart from Cat Woman, when Helen came round to my house to play, we aspired to be Men from Uncle. As far as I could see, women on TV were there either to be made fun of, like Alf Garnet's wife in Till Death Us Do Part who was always being shouted at, or for decoration, like in Bruce Forsyth's game show, with its irritating catch phrase. 'Nice to see you, to see you nice!' Bruce seemed to surround himself with grinning assistants with vacant smiles that said, 'Look at me, I've traded in my brain for a fridge-freezer, a set of luggage, a teasmaid, a cuddly teddy bear...'

Or there was the boring Miss World competition, where all the contestants lined up on stage in bathing suits. I never understood why. Where was the swimming pool? But we never did get to see them swim which might have lessened the tedium a fraction. The ubiquitous Bruce Forsyth would appear on the judging panel, presumably on the lookout for new assistants. 'Nice to see you, to see you nice! Can I interest you in a teasmaid, my lovely?' I hated all these programmes.

No, Helen and I had to content ourselves with male role models. Once Rory tired of playing with his younger sister and had school friends of his own, I would stage great dramatic productions with Helen on the nursery table. We would charge the grown-ups an entry fee for the privilege of viewing our cutting-edge drama and send the proceeds off to the World Wildlife Fund.

Luckily the charity had no idea of the seedy content of our 'kitchen sink' docu-dramas. These would revolve around some low-life criminals, alcoholics or down-and-outs, the sort of characters we had glimpsed on The Wednesday Play on TV. Angus managed to wangle a star part in one production as the policeman who comes to arrest us at the end. His negotiating hand was strengthened by the fact that he possessed a trolley on wheels. It was normally full of bricks, but if emptied and turned around, the trolley could be propelled like a scooter and used as the police car. He could also do a very convincing impression of a siren, so that swung it.

At the crucial moment in the performance, Angus sped across the floor below the stage, blaring out, 'Nee-naw, nee-naw, nee-naw!' Then to our consternation and his surprise, the trolley tipped up and crashed in front of the audience. It wasn't quite the ending we had rehearsed and it certainly wasn't Z-Cars, but the audience clapped and cheered wildly at such a dramatic climax.

* * *

For a while I went to drama classes at Bede College, a teacher training college in Durham. It was about this time, aged eight, I had my one and only big break. A former pupil of Dad's, John Irvine, was making a documentary for the BBC about the General Strike of 1926 which was sparked by the miners being locked out of work by the coalowners. Irvine enlisted some of his school friends and his old history teacher as minor characters in the film.

Dad was to be the County Durham coalowner, Lord Lambton being driven up the drive to Lambton Castle and running the gauntlet of angry miners whom he had forced out on strike.

A child was needed to sit with him in his Bentley. Strictly speaking, it should have been a boy, Lambton's son, but they decided a girl might heighten the drama. Dad put in a word on my behalf and I was chosen to be Lady Lucy.

We spent a long afternoon outside the Castle, standing about waiting to be stars. A piece of fake fur was attached to the collar of my Sunday coat and I rehearsed my part until I was word perfect.

'What are those men doing there, Daddy?' I had to say.

A bus load of miners turned up dressed in old work clothes, mufflers and caps. They looked nothing like the miners we were used to seeing at the huge parades through Durham on the annual Miners' Gala Day. A mass political rally and social day out, the Gala took place every July and from early in the morning, huge crowds would pour into the city behind their pit village brass bands and colourful banners. I used to watch in mesmerised envy as their teenage daughters ran around in huge circles ahead of the bands, chanting raucously in 'Kiss Me Quick' cowboy hats.

But on the day of filming, the pitmen were well fired up for their part of shaking fists and shouting at the bosses in the posh car. The posh car was a gleaming black Bentley owned by a vintage car enthusiast who dressed up as the chauffeur and kept nervously polishing its bonnet.

It was 1966, only forty years on from the Lockout. In 1926 most miners' families had stuck it out for six months without wages, some had not. Those that had capitulated and gone back to work were branded 'scabs' and never forgiven. Apparently old scores between the pitmen were settled during the filming, such was the bitter legacy of '26. At the time, I was blissfully unaware of the politics, yet detected an undercurrent that I mistook for the same nerves that I was experiencing.

So the scene was set. All afternoon, we drove endlessly up and down the long driveway to Lambton, a cameraman and sound recordist in a cramped heap at our feet.

The director told me, 'look scared' at the miners. 'Sound scared.'

The miners hove into view. They charged at the car. Angry faces shouted at us, fists hammered on the window. The chauffeur was wincing behind the polished dashboard. Boy, was I scared. I fluffed my lines. We did it again.

'What are those men doing there, Daddy?' I asked (convincingly frightened).

Dad looked grumpy and said nothing. He was acting like mad.

John Irvine suggested I ask another question to grumpy father. This was great, my part was expanding.

'Do you have a cousin?' Irvine asked. Many. I picked one at random.

'Ask if he's going to be at home when you get there,' instructed the director.

'Daddy,' I asked with trembling voice, 'will cousin Alastair be there for tea?'

Dad continued to scowl and say nothing. The Bentley pressed on (extremely cautiously) through the ranks of picketing miners and they shouted at the retreating car.

The footman, (a friend of Irvine's) rushed to open the car door for us. We stepped out. Dad said, 'Thank you, James,' (still grumpily).

The butler (another friend of Irvine's) came forward to take Dad's stick and hat. We disappeared into the Castle. It was high drama.

At the end of the day, I stood by the bus and watched as the pitmen climbed back on, offering sweets to a couple of them. They took the sweets, grinned and disappeared back to Ferryhill. Deep down I knew that these grubby, noisy, energetic men were the stars. Somehow, they had stolen the show.

Later, I received my fee of six guineas. This was a fortune. I was allowed to keep six shillings to spend on a record while the six pounds were put into a Post Office savings account.

Finally the night came when the documentary, *1926*, was to be shown. There was some bad news which Dad broke to me earlier in the day. The film, which was originally going to be an hour long, has been cut to half an hour. And there was some really bad news; our speaking parts had been left out. Mum tried to make the tragedy sound glamorous.

'It happens to film stars all the time - their best bits left on the cutting-room floor,' she sympathised.

The Cutting-Room Floor! It had a certain edgy professional sound to it.

I visualised film strewn over a studio floor like snips of ribbon, bits of Dad and me along with those classic lines;

Daddy, what are those men doing?

Will Cousin Alastair be there for tea?

Thank you, James.

My parents made a big thing of staying up to watch this truncated film, anyway. It was narrated by a friend of Dad's from the University. There was a lot of Mr Evans sitting on a train going places. Suddenly, flashing before our eyes, was the Bentley with a grumpy man, an anxious-looking girl and a shouting crowd. Then they were all gone and it was back to Mr Evans sitting on a train again. If we hadn't been staring unblinkingly at the screen, we probably would have missed it. It was hardly the stuff of Oscars, but at least we hadn't suffered the fate of the footman and butler who had been completely axed to pieces on the Cutting-Room Floor. And to lessen the sting of disappointment I did have the six guineas as proof of my stardom.

Careers were made and broken by that ground-breaking docu-drama. John Irvine went on to Hollywood. Dad and I went back to school.

There were other influences of popular culture that seeped into our everyday life - comics, for instance. We were allowed a weekly comic delivered with the newspapers which was fine and dandy, except being in a teacher's household, there were conditions attached to the privilege. It had to have some educational value. Don, whose room was in the attic and whose intellect was also several storeys higher than the rest of us, took *Knowledge. Knowledge* was frighteningly highbrow with earnest articles on space and machines, without a single cartoon character. Just looking at the cover could bring on a nervous headache.

For several years, I settled on *Treasure,* which was a compromise mix of frivolous stories and improving things to do and make. At some stage I managed to wangle receiving *Bunty*, that glorious collection of adventure stories for girls that fuelled my quite unrealistic expectations of boarding school and friendship groups a few years later. But in the main, comics were for holidays. Many a wet day in Scotland (where we nearly always went on holiday) was spent pouring over old copies of *The Beano, The Dandy* or *The Eagle.*

There were limits, however. Mum quietly but firmly resisted my requests to receive *Jackie* on a weekly basis. It was forbidden fruit on which the household budget would not be spent. Occasionally I was allowed to buy it with my own pocket money. Not only did it feature much sought-after pop pin-ups, but it was full of fascinating cartoon stories about older girls and their relationships.

They usually began with a girl (long flowing hair, eyelashes like small bats, lips like Mick Jagger) taking a dog for a walk. She would bump into a boy (shorter flowing hair, chin like Kirk Douglas, lips like Mick Jagger) also taking a dog for a walk. Some hiatus would follow - dog runs off or boy runs off - giving rise to a lot of misunderstanding between dog owners. Of course the reader is privy to all the angst, because it's all revealed in deliciously secretive think bubbles. It always ended with a close-up of both sets of Mick Jagger lips about to kiss, all problems resolved.

Jackie provided a heady glimpse of life beyond primary school, where boys grew up to be sensible and girls grew long legs and wore fantastic bell-bottoms. I began to grow my hair. This was not without its traumas. Mum agreed to growing it out, but insisted on cutting my fringe. Not once did she achieve a straight cut. My fringe usually looked like it had been cut with pinking shears by someone in a hurry to catch a train. I dreaded fringe cutting time. Worse still, I knew from my Go-Girl Beauty Book (free with Jackie) that hair could qualify as your crowning glory. The second most important hair care rule, after keeping it clean, was emphasised in bold type, **Don't Cut It Yourself!** The cut was the thing that could make or break a hairstyle.

It was definitely a job for an expert, so lay down those scissors! It could take months to put right if you didn't.

And so it did. By which time my fringe was ready for another appointment with Mum's cavalier wielding of the scissors. I could at least retreat to my own bedroom after surgery (I was newly promoted to a small sunny room between the nursery and my parents' room, now that Angus was out of a cot and able to share with Rory). Here I would pour over the exotic hairstyles of the Go-Girl models and the wealth of advice.

Hairstyles, it seemed, were supposed to differ depending on whether your face was round, long, square or pear-shaped; whether your chin stuck out, your nose was long or your neck short. I would contort in the mirror wondering if any of these applied to me and if they were best served by my rollercoaster fringe. There were references to perms and pincurls and chignons, about which I hadn't the first clue, but it made me feel grown-up to be reading about them.

I was especially entranced by the cartoon pictures of a woman going through her skin cleansing routine, battling with undreamed of horrors, such as oil glands, blackheads, whiteheads and clogged up pores. Personally, I thought she could have taken some advice from the chapter on hair, for she went everywhere (even to bed) with what looked like a bird's nest perched on her head.

There was an incomprehensible reference to lipstick-stained shirt collars and a strange riddle about your face being your fortune, but a lovely figure was money in the bank, too.

Apparently there was a special way of going up and down stairs and of climbing in and out of cars. Don't lunge head-first! You had to back in slowly, lowering your hips, then raise both feet and swivel your legs inside. Obviously they weren't having to contend with fighting for a seat with four brothers, or they would have realised how ridiculously impractical that suggestion was.

In fact, the only chapter that I ever put into practice was one at the end on exercises. I became quite fanatical on early morning exercising and like all new converts, was not content on doing this alone. I would bounce into Mum and Dad's bedroom at dawn and tell them brightly that it was time to get up. It must have been a small glimpse of hell to be woken in this fashion from insufficient sleep by a zealous Go-Girl. But they would struggle up without protest and submit to a routine of bending, toe-touching, leg-raising and tummy-stretching.

Dad instigated head-stands, first against the bedroom wall, then graduating to a spectacular free-standing head-stand in the middle of the bedroom. Soon the craze had swept the family and we were all capable of viewing the world from this topsy-turvy position. On one holiday on the Isle of Skye, Dad had the whole family stand on our heads against a ruined house, to surprise our friend, Ann Cunningham from Stonehaven, with whom we were picnicking.

She returned to find us all solemnly lined up on our heads waiting for her, and collapsed with laughter.

* * *

About the time I acquired the Go-Girl book I was given a Tressy doll, followed swiftly by a Cindy doll, both with the latest Sixties gear. Clothes up until then had been either for comfort or imbued with emotional significance such as kilts or the contents of the dressing up box.

My first conscious memory of clothes was having a sailor suit (at maybe three or four) which I adored and regretted growing out of as it fed my fantasies of becoming a sailor. My next was having a white cotton dress with bright red berries and a wide swishing skirt that matched one of Mum's. I recall the two of us stepping out together down Pimlico (the street that led from the safety of Caffinites to the dizzingly unmapped landscape of the town) on some now forgotten errand. Girls on the town. It was the first small frisson of womanhood.

Life was lived largely in trousers - boyish dungarees or the slim line nylon slacks from Marks & Spencer that made for easy dashing about for girls from U.N.C.L.E. Tartan pinafores or kilts were for Sunday best. Mum's home-knit jumpers and cardigans went with everything. Highly patterned anoraks, again came from M&S, one of Durham's few clothing outlets. It was that or Doggarts, the local department store which had been cutting edge in the 1930s.

As the '60s progressed, my interest in clothes grew; Cindy, Tressy and I discovered female fashion together. The seasons could be measured by the length of Mum's skirts. Each spring her hemlines were taken up another inch. For several years, the rise seemed as inevitable as the Beatles climbing the charts.

I converted quickly to the mini-skirt - we all did - for there were no skirts of other persuasions. My enduring favourites were one in French blue with a plastic belt of large gaudy Mary Quant-style flowers, and one in soft plastic faux leather.

By the time I reached ten, Mum and I were venturing into Newcastle alone and heading for C&A to kit me out in the latest styles; cerise pink trousers and matching pink and white ribbed t-shirt, minis and skinny-rib jumpers with roll necks. I was so keen on this new found form of expression that Mum speculated (hoped?) that I might one day work in the fashion industry or run my own clothing business.

One evening after leafing through the Go-Girl pocket book and in a fit of experimentation, I decided to dress up. Over my pyjamas and dressing-gown I wrapped a tartan shawl, put on all the necklaces and brooches I could find and doused myself in the contents of a miniature bottle of lavender water that someone had given me. I descended to the kitchen (as instructed, careful to keep my weight on my back leg to give the impression of floating) and made my entry.

My brothers gawped at me in fear.

'What's she doing?' one of them asked in suspicion, as if I wasn't really present. I lowered my hips slowly into a kitchen chair, raised both feet and swivelled into position.

Mum swiftly extinguished any laughs of derision, knowing how quickly I rose to my brothers' baiting.

'She's just dressing up for supper,' she said evenly, as if I came down every night dressed like the deranged Miss Havisham from *Great Expectations*. It was kind. She probably looked at me and recognised the yearnings of the dormant woman in the tomboy girl. *I Want Never Gets. Your Turn Will Come.*

After that, the *Jackie* Go-Girl Beauty Book languished in the bottom of my hanky drawer with any illusions of running a fashion house and I went back to reading *Bunty* and *The Beano*. But something of that hankering after *Jackie* comics must have stayed with me. My turn did come. Twenty years later, I was happily writing photo stories in her sister magazines, *Patches* and *Blue Jeans*.

Road to The Isles

Most summer holidays, we went on pilgrimage. Like whooper swans we flocked north, obeying the inbuilt seasonal call to return to our ancestral lands on the Isle of Skye. We covered the four hundred miles with the same urgency, noise and impatience of homing birds, but never travelled as light.

Packing for Skye was more akin to preparing for a year long trek through the Himalayas. Captain Cook probably travelled lighter on his expeditions to the South Seas. Piled up around the family car would be luggage for seven people, sleeping bags, tartan plaids, tinned food and cricket sets, teddies and candles, radios and towels, books, toffees, picnics and potties. While Dad secured a mountain of cases on the roof rack, bound in tarpaulin and lashed to the upper deck in shipshape fashion, Mum would have the impossible task of cramming everything else (including children) into steerage.

While we pranced around getting in the way or dashed inside to fetch more essential toys, she would conjure away the mound of possessions like a party magician. Into the boot or onto the back shelf would go the bulk of it, while the seats were lined with rugs and coats and the floor space was filled up with picnic baskets and potties.

Then before her final trick of spiriting seven people into the dark, sandwich-infested interior, Mum would shout; 'Go and spend a penny!'

This was the signal that we were almost ready to set sail and should all go and relieve ourselves before hours of incarceration below deck. This baffling expression rang throughout my childhood, for I could not see the connection between coins of the realm and going to the loo. Only much later in life did I hear that the euphemism originated from the time when public conveniences charged a penny entry.

Anyway, 'Go and spend a penny!' always had the effect of making me feel suddenly desperate and I'd scamper off for a final pee.

In the 1960s my parents drove Consuls and then Ford Zephyrs which appeared specially made for roving MacLeods returning to the homelands. Not only did they have a bench seat in the back (where my three older brothers sat, jostled and argued), but also one in the front. Mum and Dad would take it in turns to drive or sit with my youngest brother, Angus, on their knee. I would occupy the middle of the bench, pressed cosily between my parents, within impaling range of the gear stick. It stuck out the side of the steering column and every time we moved into fourth gear, I was in danger of being stabbed in the solar plexus with the driver's elbow. Luckily, given the twisting nature of the roads and the groaning load on board, reaching top gear did not happen frequently.

In those days, the road to the Isles cannot have differed dramatically from that experienced by the eighteenth century travellers, Dr Samuel Johnson and James Boswell. The roads still twisted and snaked their way over the Borders, plunged into the smoky haze of Auld Reekie (Edinburgh) and then on into the Highlands. Small ferries were needed to cross the Firth of Forth at Queensferry beyond Edinburgh, Loch Linnie at Ballachulish and finally the Kyle of Lochalsh to reach Skye. It was a landscape of single track roads and passing places that hugged the shoreline or clambered over precipitous mountain passes, threatening to toss our roof luggage into the glen below.

A few years later, the Highlands would echo to the sound of rock blasting as wider roads and suspension bridges made way for a new wave of tourism, but we first experienced it as inveterate travellers on an arduous expedition. The journey from the North of England to Skye took two days, with an overnight stop in Edinburgh with our Gorrie grandparents.

The one main obstacle to happiness on these journeys, apart from the boredom of playing eye-spy for several hours in a landscape of moor and sheep, was car-sickness. We never gained our sea-legs; hence the range of plastic potties in the front and back of the car. Yet sometimes the very sight of them was enough to provoke retching. As so often in our competitive household, car-sickness was made into a sport. Or rather, Dad instigated a 'colours' system of reward for each leg of the journey that we succeeded in not throwing up. To reach Edinburgh without being sick was to be awarded quarter colours; to get all the way to Skye was to earn half colours. In the unlikely event that we completed the return journey without incident, we would receive full colours. It sounded such an honour, that we did our best to achieve this heightened state of grace. But the odds were always against us.

We dreaded the decision to cross the Border using the old Roman road, via Corbridge and Otterburn, rather than the A1 coastal route or meandering across the Tweed at Coldstream. When it's a choice between Roman remains and keeping down breakfast, our enthusiasm for ancient heritage deserted us.

'Oh, not the Roman road!' we'd wail, turning green at the mere mention. 'It's a lovely route,' our parents would reply, 'straight and fast, just like the Romans laid it.'

The Romans have a lot to answer for. Their arrow-straight road rose and dipped like the sea and our stomachs heaved on each crest of the wave. With our insides travelling several miles behind us, Dad would pick this moment to light up a Woodbine and start singing Maurice Chevalier songs. This may sound over-sensitive, but Dad singing, 'Thank Heaven for Little Girls' in a French accent in a car that's rolling and pitching like a cargo ship and reeking of smoke, was guaranteed to induce nausea.

'Oh, Dad, stop singing! It's making me sick!' one of us would shout in protest, while the others clamped hands over ears and mouths and tried not to look at the blue plastic potties.

'Look at the view,' Dad would say, good-naturedly, considering the barrage of criticism his singing had just received.

And that would probably do it. Just before Otterburn lurked a metal bridge painted lime green - probably a last spiteful act from the retreating Romans - that would finally make one of us sick.

'Don't look at the bridge - !' But too late.

'Stop, I'm going to be - !'

And the car would lurch to a sickening halt. While Mum quickly bundled us out of the car, Dad would leap round to help clean up his pale shipmates with the cheerful cry of, 'Excretions Limited to the rescue!' with all the heartiness of a seasoned matelot used to swabbing decks and cleaning the 'heads'. This was a ritual repeated every couple of hours as we made our erratic progress north.

The only way to achieve quarter or half colours was to reject all food, close your eyes, attempt to sleep and refuse to play eye-spy or open your mouth for any reason other than to shout, 'Oh, stop singing, you're making me sick!'

At one stage, Dad bowed to pressure and agreed not to smoke Woodbine cigarettes in the car. But he had to smoke something, so resorted to his teenage habit of a pipe because we could tolerate the smell better. Unfortunately, the atmosphere created by the aromatic smoke was akin to a London smog and a serious hazard to driving. The experiment was abandoned and Woodies reinstated.

I would love to know what prize we would have got with full colours, but I never remember any of us achieving four consecutive potty-free trips.

* * *

The cramped tedium of these endless journeys would be broken by scheduled stops for food and ferry queues or unscheduled stops for punctured tyres and calls of nature. While Mum and I discreetly took ourselves off to the bushes, Rory had the disconcerting habit of peeing wherever the fancy took him, which was usually in front of strangers. On one occasion we pulled into a lay-by which was already occupied by another car. One moment the courting couple inside were enjoying peaceful intimacy and serene views, the next their lay-by had been invaded by the MacLeod juggernaut screeching to a halt in front and a seemingly endless stream of dishevelled tinkers piling out.

How their indignation must have turned to astonished alarm to see a young red-headed boy stroll up and nonchalantly relieve himself in front of their car in full view of their gaping faces. Even the rest of his family, who (apart from the sensitive Torq) were not easily embarrassed, thought that Rory's eagerness to share had gone too far this time. We swiftly clambered aboard and left before the lovers had time to recover, record our number-plate and contact the vice squad.

Over the years, we left our impression across the Highlands, usually at grand hotels where we children were barely tolerated, but for which Mum and Dad had an unfailing weakness. In one such country house I managed to smash my plate and insult the magnificent stuffed stags' heads by shouting loudly, 'Sheep! Sheep!'

We drew attention wherever we went. In one dining-room, a Catholic priest catching sight of our large number, came over and blessed and congratulated Mum (who was too amused and embarrassed to explain she was Presbyterian).

On another occasion and in experimental mood, one brother got his head stuck between the railings of an imposing hotel gateway. While his siblings felt that this would relieve the pressure on space in the car and prepared to leave, Mum (being more sentimental) insisted we stay until he was rescued.

A few years later, after stopping for petrol shortly before reaching Skye, I returned from the garage toilet to see the car pulling away without me. Shouting and gesticulating, I ran after it. They did stop for me, but I was sceptical of their protestations that they would have realised my absence before they reached the ferry.

There were two routes to Skye from Edinburgh; either crossing the Firth of Forth at Queensferry, up the A9 and turning left at Dalwhinnie to wind along Loch Laggan or going via Stirling, Crianlarich and on up to Glencoe and Fort William. If we travelled the former route and Dad was driving, he would attempt to make an unscheduled stop at Laggan village. This was to pay his respects to his great-grandfather, John MacLeod, who had been minister there and was buried in the churchyard.

Mum did not encourage this ancestor worship for it delayed the long journey even further. As we descended from Rannoch Moor down to the fertile glen, Laggan village and its substantial church would hove into view. Even if Mum was in a comatose state of deep sleep, as soon as Dad turned the car right at the junction instead of left, she would wake up instantly.

'What are you doing?' she would accuse.

'But you were sound asleep!' Dad would protest, awed by her anti-ancestor early warning system.

We were not particularly excited at looking at gravestones either, but any chance to unfold our limbs from the confines of the car and run around was seized upon. To judge by his tombstone, John of Laggan (just two generations removed from our MacLeod ancestors on Skye) had been a popular man.

The affectionate tribute of a sorrowing and attached
congregation and of friends who admired and loved to the
memory of a faithful pastor and true Christian
The Rev John MacLeod, minister of Laggan,
after a singularly devoted ministry and consistent life
he departed in perfect peace and trust

on 8th April, 1869, aged 63 years.

His seventeen year-old daughter, Mary, who died three years before him, and a ten year-old nephew are buried in the same plot. Early in his marriage, a son Cameron had died too.

From Laggan, John's eldest son Donald (our great-grandfather) had ventured off to Aberdeen University with a sack of meal to train as a minister too. It was the Gaelic-speaking Donald who had ended up in London, revived Crown Court Church for ex-pat Scots and founded St Columba's Church in Knightsbridge to minister to the many Scots servants living in the capital. (Over a century later, my youngest brother Angus would become minister in Donald's Pont Street kirk). Donald preached for Queen Victoria and taught Gaelic to her daughter Louisa (yet never taught it to his own children).

John of Laggan was survived by his widow, Agnes Balmain, three sons and six daughters (five of them not yet grown-up). Six years later, Agnes's two youngest teenage daughters, Jessie and Duncina, died within a month of each other. Agnes would go and stay with Donald and his family in London and put the dampeners on their Sunday afternoons. She would shut herself away in the attic on the Sabbath and read the Bible so she could not hear the wicked frivolities going on downstairs - her lively daughter-in-law, Minnie d'Estaire Roberts, playing the piano and singing hymns with her children. But perhaps it was a too painful reminder of what she had lost. There is a family portrait of Agnes in young middle-age looking a touch severe, but maybe it's just impatience at the time the artist is taking when this mother of eleven had a hundred chores to do.

Dad remembered meeting the last two surviving Laggan daughters, Aunt Jim (Jamesina) and Aunt Agnes, as very old ladies living in genteel poverty in Edinburgh. They had lost the last of their savings in the Great War. This seemed an amazing link with the ancestor who lay beneath the weathered headstone in this quiet Highland parish; my father had touched and spoken to John's Victorian daughters who had run around on this spot well over a hundred years before we had.

These days it's I who pulls the car over and makes my children pay their respects to their ancestor.

'Look, Laggan. That's where your - '

'Yea, yea - great-great-great grandfather's buried,' they humour me.

As a baby, we wheeled Amy in her pram into the church for a Sunday service to find a visiting group from Holland. From John's pulpit (where once he had preached in Gaelic) the service was delivered half in English and half in Dutch. As a bilingualist himself, I'm quite sure he would have approved.

* * *

60

Reaching the Skye ferry was a long anticipated moment for us all. We would have been singing "Over the Sea to Skye' since leaving Edinburgh, but finally the moment would come. The main crossing with Caledonian MacBrayne drive-on ferries was at Kyle of Lochalsh, but Dad liked to go a more adventurous route via Glenelg and Kylerhea in the summertime. In Kintail we would turn off onto the single track road, over a narrow hump-backed stone bridge and begin a Himalayan climb up the forested sides of Mam Ratagan.

The road twisted upwards towards the clouds, tightly coiled around the mountain. We held our breath as the car ground its way up and up, hugging the narrow road with its sheer drops away through the dark ranks of pine trees to the rocks below. Then the heart-hammering moment was over and we were dipping down into the lush green meadows of Glenelg. Past the sandy beach where in later years we would camp and onto the narrow jetty to wait for Murdo to come across the rushing currents of Kylerhea with his small ferry.

In the Eighteenth Century this was where the drovers crossed with their Black Cattle, swimming them to the mainland for the long drove down to the Lowlands and England. There the small, sturdy animals were fattened up to feed the populations of the growing towns. The Highland economy was based on cattle - and their cattle fuelled the Industrial Revolution.

Lachy Ferguson of Dunvegan recalled his drover grandfather in late Victorian times, still collecting cattle from the Outer Isles where the beasts had to be strapped to boats in rough seas for the crossing to Skye. They were de-horned at Herebost and fed up during the winter then taken on the arduous ten day drove to the sales in Stirling. Lachy's grandfather slept with the cattle (about 350) at night because drovers could not stay in the hotels. Many head of cattle were lost swimming them across the capricious waters at Glenelg.

In 1841, the circuit judge, Lord Cockburn, wrote of crossing on the ferry at Kylerhea. "This ferry though boasted the best in Skye is detestable at least for carriages. But what can a ferry be for carriages, where ours is only the third that has passed this year ..."

While we waited by our carriage, we stretched aching limbs and threw pebbles into the sea, breathing in sweet salty air and looking impatiently across at the stark umber hills of Skye, so close across the narrow bubbling water. The ferry would glide in with a whiff of diesel and a clanking of metal as the ramp dropped onto the quayside.

Dad, now wearing his kilt since crossing the border, would share a greeting and a dram with Murdo, while the ferryman waited for the five or six cars needed to fill his vessel. There would be much manoeuvring and grinding of metal as vehicles were waved on and the boat was carefully balanced with its cargo. Minutes later we were clattering off on the far jetty and pulling up the sheer slope on the Skye side.

'I need the loo!' someone would shout, just so we could stop and they could jump out and claim; 'I'm the first to touch Skye!'

For after the initial euphoria had subsided, there were still nearly two hours of driving to reach the west of the island, Dunvegan and our home at Suardal. The narrow roads wound their way out of the boggy moorland above Kylerhea, through the township of Broadford and meandered around the shoreline at the feet of the towering Cuillin range.

The ancient rounded granite Red Cuillins that belonged to the MacDonalds were dismissed as 'Slag Heaps', while we praised the mighty jagged peaks of MacLeod's Black Cuillins. Diversion would come in the shape of on-coming traffic and who would have the nerve to reverse back along the narrow road to a passing place, avoiding the hazards of boggy ditches and drops into the loch.

Onto Portree, the island's capital with its harbour held in a grasp of hills. Over to Skeabost, then Edinbane, pulling over the top to catch the first glimpse of the two flat-topped mountains of volcanic lava at Dunvegan - MacLeod's Tables! A stop at the narrow mottled stone Fairy Bridge to throw in coins for good luck and secret wishes.

On past the overgrown track that marks the old road into Dunvegan, once travelled by Johnson and Boswell on their famous tour of the Highlands in 1773. A straggle of cottages came out to greet us; the ruined church at Kilmuir and its green sward of a graveyard enriched by ancestors. Down into the village, sweeping past the Dunvegan Hotel, once teetotal for the locals, but providing a table licence for passing yachting parties in pre-war days.

All noses were pressed to the car window.

'Look, there's a boat on the loch!'

'Mrs John's house!' The first pungent whiff of peat smoke.

A hoot at Donny MacKay on his bicycle. We passed the pier end and Dunvegan House, home to the MacKenzies, with its immaculate lawn reclaimed from the bog and heather. The cricketers took a swift predatory look and then it was past. The car raced up the steep rise covered in gorse bush (the hillside would be blasted away and the road widened in 1967). The first glimpses of Sheep Island and away to Dunvegan Head were tossed up and then snatched away as the road dipped past estate cottages.

Eyes left. 'There's Rose Cottage! I think I saw Cathy Heron and one of the wild cats.'

Thick woods loomed on either side. A sudden break in them revealed a pillared gateway, surrounded by rhododendron bushes, a mysterious gate to nowhere to the passing stranger. But we knew that down its hidden driveway lay ancient Dunvegan Castle on its sea-bound rock. We anticipated football in its gardens with Dame Flora, card games of Old Maid and mouth-watering teas in its keep.

Plunging out of the woods down to the loch side again, we passed the disused stables and Doon Cottage. To the right was a glimpse of the Stewarts' Beatrix Potter garden up moss covered steps; to the left, the ruins of the old inn.

I would hold my breath in sweet anticipation for the rattle, clunk, rattle of the rickety cattle grid. Round the corner to the roaring greeting of the waterfall. Up the hill to a precipitous bend where, looking back, the castle could be seen for the first time. Its grey walls and tower glimmered in the evening sun, pale gold light washed the sea. Below, seals slipped from rocks into the water and surfaced in the Suardal inlet where later I would learn to swim. A sheep's bleat carried for miles.

At last we rounded the bend and the clump of wind-blasted trees appeared that marked where the track to Suardal began. We piled out and walked, so the car stood more of a chance of escaping laceration from the stony drive that looked like a dry riverbed. Racing ahead, we climbed to the brow of the hill and then rushed forward. Sheep scattered.

'Suardal!' we screamed in delight as the stone ruin of our ancestral home emerged and greeted us with its gaping toothless smile, a rowan growing from one gable end like wiry hair.

Next to it, nestling on the site of its ancient garden was its younger relation, a wooden bungalow, built recently by my parents. Shutters had to be unlatched from the large windows, the car unpacked before the midges ate us alive, the Rayburn stoked into life, a fire lit in the large open-plan sitting-room and mattresses dragged out of bedrooms and aired. We rushed around banging open cupboards re-discovering comics and games forgotten since the last visit. (In later years, Freda of Doon Cottage would have magically prepared rooms, built a fire and arranged jugs of wild flowers to welcome us).

Eventually some of us were washed and all were fed a fry up of sausage and beans and eggs that Mum had magicked out of the small hot kitchen. Outside, clouds of midges danced in the copper sunset. Candles were fixed into holders and paraffin lamps prepared before it grew any darker ('the electric' will not come to the Claigan peninsula till the Seventies). For that night, the first night at Suardal, we would all camp by the fire on the toasting mattresses, while our parents lay on the pull-out sofa. An older brother would get the single sofa, but it was cosier to be nearer the fire, wriggling in a sleeping bag.

The curtains were drawn against an indigo sky, where bats wheeled around the ruined gables. Mum read a story, then the hissing lamps were turned off and we struggled to stay awake in the firelight. If we closed our eyes we could still feel the motion of the car.

But tomorrow we would stretch our legs and run around the ruined township. Tomorrow, we would scramble among the homes and rigs of our ancestors; we would play football where their cattle grazed.

Pastry and The Devil

Suardal may have been a picturesque family cabin, but life here was no 'Little House on the Prairie' idyll. We would wake to the shrill blast of a bosun's whistle, rudely summoning us out of sleeping bags and bunks. There would stand Dad, with his hair tousled like Kenneth Moore in The Cruel Sea, looking disgustingly cheerful at action stations. At this point we would brace ourselves for his raucous maritime morning call.

'Eave-o! Eave-o! Lash up and stow!

Show leg, show leg!

Sun's up over the yardarm, burning your eye-balls out!

Eave-o! Eave-o!'

Groans of protest would be drowned out by a further ear-piercing blast on the whistle. There was never any point in diving for cover, because the whole noisy routine would be repeated until we'd swung our legs over our hammocks and shown him our eyeballs.

Scampering along to the mess deck, breakfast would come as a blessed relief to the senses. While Captain Bligh went to shave outside, we would tuck into Mum's lumpy porridge or a bowl of cereal. Either way, it would have a distinctive piquancy not experienced in the soft south where daily milk bottle deliveries were the norm. Skye milk would invariably be on the turn. But then it was a major feat getting it to the table at all.

Before leaving Durham, Dad would ring through to the MacDonald's farm at Uiginish across the loch from Dunvegan to alert them to our coming. To him, that call to the cheerful, Gaelic-speaking Annabel and Al MacDonald would herald the beginning of the holidays after a busy school term. It gave him the same sense of well-being and anticipation as listening to the shipping forecast tell of conditions around the Hebrides. It would also trigger milk deliveries after our arrival.

On certain days of the week, a large silver churn of milk would be left at the garage in Dunvegan village three miles away, for us to collect. If we were lucky, the day would be overcast or rainy. If not, the milk would have been warming up nicely and would already have a sour taste by the time we got it home. But sour milk was a holiday taste and one we soon adapted to, along with the ritual of burnt toast. There was no more comforting sound than that of Mum's tuneful humming at the kitchen sink, accompanied by the brisk scraping of overdone toast.

Sometimes, in the lull after eating, there would be a reading and a prayer. Our eighteenth century ancestor, old Donald, who had dwelt in the now ruined Suardal, had been the first in the area to introduce family prayers. Although himself a farmer-warrior and sword-maker to the MacLeod chief, he educated his sons and the eldest, Norman, became a Church of Scotland minister. Thus began a distinguished line of ministers descending from the house of Suardal, both from Norman and from second son, Donald, our direct ancestor. That was until my father broke the mould and went into teaching (after a spell in the Navy and winning the war with Churchill).

Both our parents were deeply spiritual. Dad, a lover of Burns' poetry, once spoke of how the young poet was influenced by his parents' practice of family worship. It was very much his own belief.

'The parents believe they are plaiting a life-line,' he said, 'which they hope their children will grasp hold of for the rest of their lives, however far they may wander from home.'

We would take it in turns to do the reading, while Mum would say prayers in a clear, tranquil voice that would momentarily be-calm her restless flotilla of children. Then, our stomachs satisfied and our souls tended to, the aim would be to slink away and escape outside while Mum and Dad sat on smoking a sociable Woodbine.

Because we knew it was a matter of minutes before the dreaded order came. 'Chores!' one of our parents would cry and put a halt to playtime. For the lack of 'mod cons' in this rural retreat meant that half the morning seemed to be taken up with jobs. Given our propensity to argue among ourselves over who did what, it might have taken a lot longer, but Mum swiftly assigned our chores and quelled any demarcation disputes like the best of shop stewards.

Dad and the older boys were the elite of the workforce - the union of firemen and boiler makers. While Dad stoked up the Rayburn, Don and Torq took it in turns to refill the paraffin lamps, trim the wicks and clean the glass funnels. Each bedroom had candles in Wee Willie Winkie holders that needed restocking by melting the bottom of the new candle onto the top of the old. We younger ones were the unskilled labourers. There was the table to clear, floor to sweep, a monumental amount of washing up, drying and putting away to accomplish. Someone would get out the carpet sweeper and push it back and forth, or more likely stand on it and sing (using the long handle as a microphone) until spotted and informed upon. If we were lucky, we got to do the 'coaling'. This was a transitional chore between the highly skilled and the casual, and apprenticeships were greatly fought over. It entailed going out to the coal heap behind the house and shovelling spadefuls into two coal scuttles. One fed the ever hungry Rayburn, source of cooking and hot water, while the other was for the coal fire in its trendy free-standing chimney stack dividing the large sitting-room from the dining area.

Coaling offered a higher status to washing up. It got you outside and allowed hands to get satisfyingly dirty enough to show that a hard job had been done. It was usually accompanied by loud grunts and exaggerated groans to draw maximum attention and praise. It would finish with a dramatic stagger to the back door with a bucketful of coals, which would be dumped down with a triumphant look that said;

'See, there, you soft soap-suddy lot! I've dug those out with my own bare hands!'

Apart from the Rayburn and open Baxi fire, there was no other heating in the house. But the large picture windows welcomed in any sunshine and on sunny days, the house sizzled like a greenhouse.

As chief fireman it was Dad's job to rake out the embers, deposit the bucket of ash in any of the numerous potholes along the track and lay a new fire for the evening. To help us along he would sing songs about dubious sailors called Frankie and Johnny, or do his Maurice Chevalier impression which was guaranteed to speed up production. But there was no alternative entertainment. Transistor radios were of little use, as they picked up virtually nothing during the daytime.

Strangely, at night, we could pick up all manner of international fare, most of it unwelcome. We would twiddle around for ages trying to find anything that resembled decent music (which to us meant pop) with little success.

Fiddle, twiddle, crackle. Someone yodelling to himself would be replaced by rousing Bavarian folk music. Swish, crackle, whine. French DJs talking endlessly and never playing any music. Twiddle, fizz. An Italian opera singer belting out in mid aria. Fiddle, crackle. Then joy! DJ. Stuart Henry would burst through the ether on 208 medium wave from Radio Luxembourg for half a Rolling Stones' record and then fizzle out again. Inexplicably, he would be superseded by some sugary-sweet choral group, like the Swingle Singers on the Light Programme, crooning the type of melodies our parents could sing along to. This came to be known disparagingly as 'Ugh! Radio Two Music', always said with a down-turn of the mouth and a half-retching noise. A frantic turn of the dial and it was almost a relief to find the Bavarians again, who by this time sounded like they had broken into a beer cellar and were louder and more raucous than ever.

So Dad's rendition of Frankie and Johnny in the morning was fine by comparison. Finally we would be free to play outside on the hillside or among the wind blasted tree stumps down the track, while our parents carried on working.

Washing must have been the heaviest of chores. It all had to be done by hand, using an old washboard as scrubber. Mum would pound away in the sink, scrubbing and rinsing, then pass the wet piles through the window for Dad to put them through the hand-ringer outside. After this exhausting procedure, they would be hung on the line to dry (the washing, not my parents). Mum's only abiding memory of their first summer 'holiday' at Suardal in 1959, was endless lines of white nappies flapping in the breeze.

'I never sat down all holiday,' she recalled, in a tone that gave no hint of nostalgia for those days before electricity.

* * *

Catering presented another challenge, not only for the hungry brood of

MacLeods fresh off the hill or football pitch, but for relations, neighbours, stray campers and unexpected visitors who found their way to our remote home. On Skye it was always best to expect the unexpected. We weren't on the telephone and the mail arrived in the late afternoon, so the only advanced early warning system was from one of us scouts on the hill, spotting approaching walkers or occasional cautious cars.

My parents' afternoon snooze would often be shattered by cheerful cries of, 'Hello, Sir!' as a wave of old boys from Durham School breached the remote hilltops and poured down into Suardal's secluded glen. Mum's heart would sink at the invasion. 'Oh!' she would sigh at the realisation that they could never truly get away from the job. Then, being the professional actress and entertainer that she was, she would go out to greet them and somehow magic up enough food to feed whoever came.

As we grew older, we became privy to the conjuring tricks in the kitchen. For a time, there was only one grocery shop in the village, so Mum relied heavily on tinned and packet foods - soups, dried mashed potato, instant whip pudding mixes. Nothing was wasted. If some child dropped the precious 'fluffy' pud on the carpet, it was swiftly scraped up and served with a flourish. If resources were scarce, a coded message would go out with whispered urgency, 'Family Hold Back!'

On one occasion, we had friends from the village out for a meal, Charlie and Cathy Heron. Charlie, an Aberdonian, was the retired butler at Dunvegan Castle and as a young man had met and married local girl, Cathy who was a maid to the chiefly family. They brought friends with them who were visiting from Aberdeen, with their son who was working in London. Word had it, he was doing rather well in catering.

Things were going swimmingly - drams and good conversation, soup and the main course nearly over - when someone asked Iain what it was he actually did in London.

'I'm the pastry chef at The Savoy,' he admitted with a bashful smile.

There was an audible in-take of breath around the table. Even we had heard of The Savoy. It was famous, high-class, and renowned for its teas and pastries. Mum didn't bat an eyelid as we cleared the plates and regrouped in the kitchen for serving out the pudding.

Well it was pastry based - plate size apple and mince pies - but that was where the similarity to The Savoy ended. They were a hasty purchase from the village of unknown origin. Still there was plenty of tinned cream to go round and lift the taste. Mum was not going to be daunted by having a world class pastry chef sitting beside her at table. In MacLeod philosophy, it was less about what you ate, than the spirit in which you ate it, that counted. Hospitality ranked higher than haute cuisine.

Pieces of pie began to be carved up and sent out to our discerning diners. It was at this point that Mum gave a startled little yelp.

'What's wrong?' I asked.

'It's mince!' she gasped. We peered closer in confusion. 'It's not sweet mince - it's mince!'

Mum was staring hard at the offending pie as if willing it to turn back into the mincemeat of her dreams. But there was no getting away from it - this pie was a savoury meat pie.

For a moment we stood around opening and closing our mouths like fish, then Mum took command of her paralysed shoal.

'Make sure all the guests have apple pie in front of them,' she hissed, 'quickly!'

We scuttled back into the room and did a quick check. Thankfully, so far they had opted for apple. All except Dad, that was. He was holding forth at the top of the table, quite oblivious to the culinary time-bomb in his bowl.

We retrieved the other rogue pieces of mince pie and reported back. 'It's okay - apart from Dad.'

'Well bring his back,' Mum said.

'But he's already putting cream on it!' we whispered, trying to smother small squeaks of laughter.

Mum glanced through the kitchen door in alarm. There was no way of alerting him without the terrible secret of the Suardal pastry crisis being exposed to one of London's top chefs. She rolled her eyes and gave a shrug as if to say, Dad might not notice. Dad was not renowned for his discerning palate and on holiday was more interested in a leisurely drink while his food grew cold. But surely this would leave even his taste buds gastronomically challenged?

We looked at Mum for our lead.

'Family Hold Back,' she said briskly and divided up tiny slivers of apple pie for the rest of us.

We returned and Mum took up the conversation where she had left off, as if the emergency in the kitchen had never been. But try as we might, we couldn't keep our eyes off Dad and his reaction, if any, to meat pie and Carnation cream. It held a horrible fascination, like going to witness a public execution. We all felt bad about leaving him to his lonely fate at the end of the table, but couldn't wait to see him take his first mouthful.

Dad being a slow eater, we were almost in a frenzy of anticipation by the time he started munching. In it finally went. He stopped momentarily, a puzzled look on his face. He glanced around the table. Quickly looking away, I concentrated hard on making my piece of pie last as long as possible. By the time I shot him another furtive look, Dad was once again tackling his pudding. It was almost unbearable to watch.

He didn't finish it, but he didn't rush to the sink and throw-up either. He was a team player to the end. So a pastry scandal that could have rocked the nation was averted and the guests went away none the wiser.

'What was in that pie?' Dad asked afterwards. It took several minutes before anyone could stop their hysterical laughter long enough to explain.

* * *

Frequent forays outside the Suardal glen were needed to replenish stocks. After about a week, we were adapted to the country and our view of what was big and exciting subtly altered. Trips to the village shop were referred to as going 'down-town'.

It was a pretty heady experience after roaming the hillsides like fugitives in the heather or playing around the house for hours on end. So if someone said, 'I'm going down town to the shops, want to come?' we were there like a shot.

And shops was strictly speaking, true. Apart from Anna MacLean's grocery store with its high wooden counter and towering stacked shelves behind, there was MacKay's hardware shop at the other end of the village. Housed in the long room of the old school house, built in 1878, this Aladdin's cave of odds and ends was presided over by the MacKay brothers. It was dark, wooden and creaky, bathed in sepia light, with a counter that seemed to stretch off into infinity. It smelt of polish and paraffin and sold everything from Wellington boots to string. The highlight was rummaging through the curling postcard collection while our parents chatted to the Mssrs MacKay about life and the weather. These cards depicted the village in a monochrome era of thatched roofs and steamboats, when Model T Fords parked outside the Dunvegan Hotel and houses weren't whitewashed.

One elderly resident remembered when there were no shops. Once a week, Samuel MacDonald would come round on a horse-drawn cart selling bread. The rest of the week they made their own scones and oatcakes. People bought sacks of meal and flour or brought their own oats to be ground at the mill. Others had their wages partly paid in meal. Fishermen with an extra barrel of herring bartered it for another crofter's excess potatoes. In the early twentieth century wages were low, diets restricted and there was little sign of a cash economy.

Despite this, Dunvegan grew into a teaming metropolis for the surrounding area, with a hotel, boarding house, bank, golf course and club, two churches, customs and excise officer, coastguard, secondary school and a thriving pier. This link by sea, up the island-studded loch to the Minch, was the community's umbilical cord to the world beyond, and had been since the dawn of time. Ancient brochs studded the coastline, built over 2000 years ago to fend off raiders from the sea. This was the way the Vikings arrived and colonised the area, establishing their stronghold on Dunvegan's sea-bound rock. The sons of Leod came and went from their fortress by a sea gate - Dunvegan Castle had no access by land until the eighteenth century.

By the early 1900s, there were regular steamers from the Clyde bringing coal, provisions, mail, passengers and gossip to Skye and on to the Outer

Isles. Boats called daily except on Sunday and trips went out to farthest flung St Kilda throughout the summer. The S.S *Dunara Castle* and S.S *Hebrides* still called weekly until 1961, when the owners, MacBrayne, changed over to road haulage. Apart from a few fishing boats, trade by sea died off and the once bustling pier fell into disrepair. Passengers arrived by motor bus.

Even in the early '60s, most of the visitors at this time were the coach loads of returning islanders during the two week summer holidays from Glasgow and Edinburgh. In Glendale alone, four packed buses would bowl into the remote glen on the far side of Loch Dunvegan. Two or three homes in the village were taking in boarders, but the proliferation of B&Bs was yet to come.

The Dunvegan Hotel had been established at the turn of the twentieth century as a 'dry' hotel. The chiefly landlord of the day, Norman Magnus, had been so concerned with the level of hard drinking among his tenants and the poverty exacerbated by wages being poured over the bar, that he declared his estates teetotal.

Too often he saw the mail coach and horses tethered outside the hotel, where the frozen and drenched postie was thawing out after a perilous seven hour journey over the hills from Portree. One local man told me that in the end the hotel lost its licence after a stabbing incident. Norman Magnus encouraged a man called Budge, a commission agent around the Western Isles, to take on the hotel. Budge, against all village predictions, proved that a Highland hostelry could be run without a bar and did so for over thirty years. The guest books show a varied clientele; in 1914 commercial travellers ate alongside Count Herndorff from Vienna, members of the Bachelors' Club of Piccadilly and six officials from the Scottish Land Court settling disputes. In 1927 there were visitors from Texas, New Zealand and Baghdad as well as representatives of the National Association for the Prevention of TB.

But MacLeod of MacLeod's fervour for temperance may have been influenced by more personal encounters. Local legend puts the blame on a handsome drunk called Alastair. He had fallen into a ditch by the side of the road. Norman Magnus stopped to rescue him and help him out, only to be met with the protest, 'Move on MacLeod, my rent's paid!'

On another occasion, when the landlord was showing a visitor around, Alastair gave them a more startling greeting. He spun around and lifted his kilt with a jaunty cry, 'Aye, and I'm handsome from the back too!'

To offer more orthodox diversions, chief Norman Magnus endowed the village with a gathering hall. This was a revolutionary idea. Socialising was largely done in people's houses, where they would 'ceilidh' (get together to recount the old stories and sing songs). In the 1900s, there were still many 'black houses' - thatched stone dwellings with a barn attached, with a central peat fire and a hole in the roof for the smoke to escape. That was the theory. In practice, in windswept Skye, the smoke would go everywhere but through the roof and it could take several minutes before a visitor could work out where he was and who was there. It was not until the advent of government grants to upgrade housing that thatched houses were abandoned.

The men of Dunvegan would also gather at the smithy or cobbler's - known as the village 'parliament' - to discuss the news in the three day old newspapers that came by mail from Glasgow or the weekly *Highland News* which was only two days old. Sharing a pinch of snuff or passing around a pipe of tobacco, there would be much debate about politics, especially land and its ownership in an area where land tenure was still feudal. During the First World War, news was posted every midday in the windows of the post office, for many of the local men were territorials and had gone off to fight.

A village hall was controversial from another point of view - that of the strictly Sabbatarian Free Church and its more fundamentalist off-shoot the Free Presbyterians. Even into modern times, the FPs saw a village hall as an instrument of the Devil that might encourage dancing and music - further instruments of the Devil. They had reason to be fearful, for one local man recalled fondly the seasonal influx of Irish herring girls who enlivened the village dances. 'When the hall got hot,' he said, 'everything smelt of herring.'

Meanwhile, the Ladies and Gentlemen players of Dunvegan Golf Club were augmenting club funds by holding concerts with dances to follow.

But opposition to musical entertainment did not stop. In the mid-Sixties, the Scottish Trio, who were going to bring their classical music to Dunvegan, were cancelled after the Free Church minister preached against them bringing "the work of the Devil" to the village.

Not to be outdone, the firebrand Free Presbyterian minister, Colhoun, preached against the corrupting influence of those most militant and subversive of revolutionaries who used the hall, the Women's Rural Institute. What did he imagine went on at such meetings? Jam smuggling? The idea of women meeting together to socialise unsupervised was just too explosive.

'There's a Devil going through Dunvegan with WRI written on its tail!' he thundered out his warning in Glendale, where there was no village hall to tempt the local women to meet together in such a depraved way.

Nevertheless, by this time, Norman Magnus's hall had long been in use for wicked dances, cubs, brownies, badminton, whist drives, a lending library, occasional film show and the monthly rave-up with the WRI. The decadence didn't stop there. For a short time in 1980, the Church of Scotland (which had no hall of its own) used the village hall on the Sabbath to gather after the morning service. One elderly woman from the Free Church was in a lather of excitement about this development and could not wait to question me.

'What did you do in there?' she asked with that wide-eyed expectancy normally associated with children and Santa Claus.

I shrugged. 'Just drank coffee and chatted.'

Her look of disappointment haunts me still.

Norman Magnus's teetotal legacy was not so lasting. In the 1950s, the chiefly landlord of the day, Dame Flora, embarked on a mission to stimulate the down-at-heel post-war economy with tourism. She introduced Skye Week, a series of events in May to try and extend the short tourist season and she successfully encouraged MacLeods from all over the world to return to their home in Dunvegan and search for their roots. Although a non-drinker herself, the area went 'wet' again. The Dunvegan Hotel became licensed and the bank was turned into The Misty Isle Hotel with a public bar.

While tourism and seasonal work picked up momentum, many services - bank, library, secondary schooling - drifted away across the island to the capital, Portree. Services were provided centrally, making forays back to outposts like Dunvegan. Fish, meat, books and money could all be had from travelling vans on certain days of the week. Post vans carried passengers, bus drivers collected shopping for isolated housewives. On one famous occasion when my parents had missed the travelling bank, the obliging driver and employee of the Royal Bank of Scotland drove out to Suardal and transacted business parked outside the house.

This spirit of co-operation and the lack of concern about time or sticking to bothersome schedules were deep-rooted traditions on an island cut off by the sea and frequently battered by Atlantic gales and rain. One intrepid MacLeod couple, Toni and Kenneth, were lured from London at the end of the Second World War, by an invitation to stay with Dame Flora at Dunvegan Castle. They took a sleeper to Fort William, a further train to Mallaig, a ferry to Armadale in the south of Skye, then a bus to Sligachan and finally Dunvegan.

Any jadedness from the long journey was banished when the bus began to race a Morris Minor carrying four men in black and a coffin in the front seat. The bus won, only because the funeral party stopped off for drams before delivering the coffin to the church.

Safely ensconced at the Castle, the MacLeod visitors were encouraged to take the bus to Portree for an outing and return for dinner at eight in the evening. With rationing still in place, petrol was scarce and the obliging bus driver stopped at many a gate to pick up a shopping basket with shopping list and money for marooned households. Having done their sight-seeing in the small harbour town, Toni and Kenneth climbed back on the bus before six o'clock, along with the other passengers, a mountain of shopping baskets, several dogs and a calf. Nothing happened. The driver was waiting to meet the steamer from the mainland.

But the boat was late coming in, so all the passengers piled off again and adjourned to the bar of the Royal Hotel (the site of MacNab's inn where the fugitive Bonnie Prince Charlie said farewell to Flora MacDonald in 1746). When the boat finally docked, the bus filled up once more and set off on the 23 miles back to Dunvegan. Halfway over, the bus made a stop at the small township of Edinbane. This was the site of an old posting house and the first place on Skye to sell liquor legally.

In time honoured tradition, the men disembarked and headed into the bar. Presumably knowing they were here for some time, another passenger took the opportunity to visit a friend in the small cottage hospital. When the drinkers re-emerged and heard of this, they all decided they must go at once and visit the patient too. So off they piled once more and went to give solace to the sick.

By the time the crammed but jovial busload eventually trundled into Dunvegan, it was almost eight. Tony and Kenneth ran the final mile to the Castle, worried at how late they were. There was Dame Flora already dressed for dinner and waiting to welcome them. She waved aside their apologies and tales of the tardy bus with amusement.

'Oh, I knew the bus would be late,' she said unperturbed. 'It hasn't been on time since the bus driver stopped courting my parlour maid!'

* * *

One of the enterprising retailers who roamed around the Highlands in the '60s was a Pakistani from Glasgow called Kaliq. In his mobile shop he brought clothing and household goods to the shop-starved populations of scattered island townships and they bought with enthusiasm. So much so, that Kaliq was able to take over the premises of the old MacKay brothers in the village, set up a permanent shop and marry local woman, Jessie.

The Kaliqs' emporium made going 'down-town' a seriously hedonistic experience. They sold everything; coats, Cornflakes, batteries, baps, toys, tumblers, comics, cosmetics, soap, soups, plastic containers, potatoes and postcards in glorious Technicolor.

We still shopped at Anna's too, for she allowed my parents to run up a 'slate' during the holiday and supplied Dad with non-tipped cigarettes which she kept in a secret drawer. These were produced with a furtive flourish, like contraband that was in short supply and had been smuggled in especially for hardened filter-spurning seadogs. Usually it was *Players* with a picture of a sailor on the packet (obviously Dad) or if he was extremely lucky and well-behaved, a precious consignment of *Woodbines*.

In later years, milk would arrive spasmodically in cartons from mainland dairies at Dingwall and Anna would keep some of this liquid gold for us. The milk would come in during the afternoon and a tradition developed of Dad 'going for the milk' in the early evening. By a strange coincidence, this often coincided with his nephew, John, (also a school teacher with a cottage near the village at Roag) needing to dash down 'for the milk' at the same time. It just so happened that Anna's shop was almost next door to the Misty Isle Hotel and its bottled refreshment, dispensed by hospitable MacLeod owners. Whereas we children fell for the bogus milk run every time, Mum and John's wife Susan (who were sceptical about coincidences) knew it was a run ashore. But as long as they returned with milk at the end of the expedition, no one was forced to walk the plank.

So our craving for the bright lights and shopping would be assuaged. We had been to the land of milk and money. We had smelled the crisp pound notes in the intimate travelling bank, gawped at the treasures in Kaliq's bazaar and grown restless over empty lemonade glasses in the Misty's bar. There was only one excitement left before returning to the homestead. Dumping the rubbish.

I have a very early memory of driving close to a precipitous cliff edge on the scenic stretch of loch side between the Castle and the Suardal inlet where we sometimes swam. From this dizzy height, the rubbish was hurled over the side. We listened to the satisfying waterfall of tin cans and bottles cascading onto the colourful 57 Varieties of rocks below. There was no municipal refuse collection until the 1970s. Yet at some stage before the enlightened '70s, someone must have got agitated about the environmental consequences of throwing rubbish into the tide. For a dump was sited deep inside the woods behind the Castle, up a lonely track infested with midges. I never really took to this furtive tipping of waste after the drama of the cliff tops.

But all messages completed, we turned our back on the sophistication of tarmacadam roads and city life and headed up our pitted dirt track towards the welcoming spirals of chimney smoke. Like returning prodigals, we were eager to swap the hectic pace of downtown Dunvegan and its devilish temptations for the sanctuary of Suardal. The fatted calf awaited (or at least corned beef and mash), a story from Mum by lamplight and maybe even half a minute of Radio Luxembourg before the candles were blown out. Heaven indeed.

Picnics and Massacres

There were times when we ventured beyond the safety of the Suardal glen. In more temperate climes, such trips might have been called outings or picnics. On rugged Skye they were raised to the status of 'expeditions'. This was partly owing to the length of time it took to prepare supplies, pack rugs, cricket sets, swimming gear and extra clothing, then rally everyone off the hill or out of the loo.

Luckily, summer days in the Hebrides are long and daylight hours plentiful. I suppose this must have been an advantage to clan raiders throughout the centuries and it certainly was to our small marauding band. Often such expeditions across the island could take two hours of driving before we got anywhere, especially if we were venturing into forbidden MacDonald Country.

We had been taught from an early age that the MacDonalds were the main enemies of the MacLeods. This was perplexing as my mother was a Gorrie and therefore of the MacDonald clan. Clearly my parents' marriage must have been the result of some huge clan oversight.

But Dad had a neat, if startling, excuse. 'We either fought them or married them,' he said, as if this were the most logical of explanations.

Mum had no such hang-ups about the MacLeods. She was endlessly tolerant of 'MacLeodary', that excessive boastfulness and bonhomie of a clan that thinks itself the most important, not only in the area, but worldwide. It can't have been easy.

There had, however, been a hitch early on during their engagement when she discovered her future mother-in-law was a Campbell. Now MacDonalds cannot abide Campbells. Ever since 1692 when Campbells betrayed the rules of Highland hospitality by murdering their hosts the MacDonalds of Glencoe on behalf of the government, relations have been as icy as the snows in which they died.

Having discovered a Campbell in the camp, my parents' wedding was in danger of being called off. But Norman being a resourceful historian, went and sought the help of Sheila's great-aunt, Amy Cameron, the family genealogist.

'Find me a Campbell in Sheila's family!' Norman pleaded. 'And quickly.'

I imagine the nights were sleepless until Aunt Amy came up trumps. It took a trawl of five generations in the female line, but there she discovered the eighteenth century Grizel Campbell. There was written - or at least stitched - proof. A child's sampler embroidered by Grizel had survived since the 1740s. Sheila could no longer use the Campbell card as good reason why they should not be lawfully joined together and the marriage went ahead without bloodshed.

Often our trips out would be to places of MacLeod celebration or veneration. We would climb MacLeod's flat-topped Tables where the great sixteenth century chief, Alastair Crotach (Alastair of the humped back), had feasted King James V of Scotland, claiming the night sky as his star-studded ceiling and his torch-holding clansmen as the most precious of candlesticks. We would be taken to ruined remains of churches or strongholds, brochs or houses and clamber around moss-covered stones while Dad recounted the clan stories of heroics and sacrifice.

No story stood out more starkly in our childish memories than the gory mass murder at Trumpan church in Waternish. Forget video nasties, we had tales of medieval atrocities that would have kept Martin Scorsese awake at night.

Imagine a peaceful Sunday morning in the sixteenth century and a thatched church packed with the faithful - MacLeods of course - their chanting lifting on the breeze, mingling with the cries of seabirds on the nearby cliff-tops. But unseen by the devout, godly MacLeods were the approaching longboats of treacherous, unholy MacDonalds, slipping across The Minch and anchoring in the bay below.

The MacLeods were so wrapped in their prayers and devotion that they were taken completely by surprise. Only when the bloodthirsty enemy besieged the church, baying for them to come out, did the MacLeods realise the hopelessness of their situation. The horrific choice was either to come out and be cut to pieces or stay in the church and be burned alive. Courageously they chose to stay on, singing and praying, as the MacDonalds put their flaming torches to the thatch. I imagined the flames leaping over their heads, the screaming, the roof caving in and burning them alive.

Dad would stand among the weathered gravestones in the wind and point accusingly out to sea with his cromach (shepherd's crook) in the direction of the Outer Isles. It was almost possible to see the ghostly, fast moving galleys of the invading MacDonalds. By this time I would be in a lather of righteous indignation and anxiety. How could these murderers be so cowardly and sly as to catch people unawares like that? It was so unsporting. And why weren't they all at Church themselves? So un-Christian. But they were clever, devilishly clever.

Then Dad moved around the ruined building to the far gable end. And while we sheltered in its shadow from a westerly squall, he pointed up to a narrow slit of a window still visible in the ancient stone wall. It was about the size of a cricket bat.

'But there was one brave MacLeod who escaped,' he told us. We knew what was coming, but held our breath anyway. 'A young woman called Mary squeezed herself out of this window - but at a terrible cost. It was so narrow that it tore off one of her breasts.'

Every time I looked up at this window I winced. This horror above all others plagued my girlish mind. Brave Mary, determined to escape to save her family and friends, to warn her other kinsfolk, to save the clan. She managed to get away. She raised the alarm and word spread quickly back to Dunvegan and the chief. But she lost so much blood that she died. Heroine Mary gushing with blood, life seeping out of her, staining the springy turf around Trumpan. Mary, my own middle name.

I gazed at the window and tried to imagine if I would have managed to squeeze through. Did she climb through head or feet first? How was she not spotted? There must have been smoke and confusion everywhere, people running out screaming and on fire into the arms of the slaughterers. The MacDonalds were not so clever after all, only guarding the doorway, not expecting anyone to escape any other way and certainly not by the slip of a window above the high altar.

But my worst thought of all (and one I couldn't share with anyone, least of all my brothers) was, what had happened to the breast? Where was that bleeding appendage that caused Mary to die? It was so unfair that she got away but couldn't live because she didn't have her breast. I hugged my flat chest, feeling queasy.

Luckily the story then took an upturn. The MacLeods over at Dunvegan decided that drastic measures were needed and unfurled their greatest treasure, the magical Fairy Flag. They were few in number as the call to arms was still spreading, but once the flag was waved it appeared as if there were scores of them coming to avenge the massacred church-goers. A fierce battle was fought in which the MacDonalds were routed. They turned and fled for their boats, but these had been set adrift by the locals. The MacLeods pursued them and cut them to pieces by the shore. So many were killed that they piled up the bodies behind a dyke (wall) and pushed the dyke on top of them. Ever after they referred to the victory as The Battle of the Spoiled Dyke.

And just to cap it all, a handy witch popped up and put a curse on the one boat-load of fleeing MacDonalds that managed to cut loose and row away. A storm soon rose up and sank them, so that none of the attackers made it back to North Uist. Well it served them right for such a godless act, we thought with bloodthirsty satisfaction.

There were other attractions at the haunted Trumpan, this medieval adventure playground for active MacLeod children. A four foot high pillar called the Trial Stone - we called it the witch's stone - stood among the ancient gravestones (perhaps a pre-Christian standing stone or early grave marker). On its lichen covered face was a large pockmark, a hole into which you had to, with eyes closed, try and place your finger to ensure you go to Heaven.

Eyes screwed up, arm outstretched, we advanced over uneven ground towards the stone, plunging our fingers into the hole (often repeatedly until we arrived at the right moral verdict).

'Look, I did it!' the successful saint-to-be would cry.

'You cheated, you were peeking!' siblings instantly accused.

Mum's scarf was borrowed as a blindfold.

On bad days, some of us not only completely missed the hole, but staggered past the stone itself, arm flailing about in mid-air, a sure candidate for Hell's fire. A quick guilty look round to see if anyone else had witnessed the impending damnation, then a hurried backtrack to start all over again.

We were taken to another corner of the kirkyard to hear a further spine-chilling tale of betrayal, incarceration and madness. In the shadow of the ruined church stood a plain, mottled tombstone. The grave beneath contained the remains of the hapless Rachel Erskine, wife of the eighteenth century Jacobite, Lord Grange. He was a Jekyll and Hyde character, pious by day, debauched by night. Fearing Rachel might let slip that he was plotting with fellow Jacobites, her ruthless husband had her kidnapped and imprisoned on St Kilda, the remotest of the Western Isles, and then, bold as brass, held a mock funeral and feigned deep mourning. Lady Grange, used to the genteel life of Edinburgh was confined to her rocky fortress for seventeen years and, quite understandably, went mad. When finally she did die for real, Lord Grange, bizarrely held a second mock funeral with a coffin full of stones, while Rachel's body was smuggled to lonely Trumpan and buried with great secrecy. Only years later was the grave given its stark memorial.

R.I. P. Rachel, wife of The Hon. James Erskine,
Lord Grange, Died Aug. 1749.

With our heads reeling from such X-certificate stories, it's a wonder we slept at night.

To calm the nerves, there was always the magic stone font for light relief. This roughly carved bowl nestling in Trumpan church, though far from modern plumbing or taps, was always full of water. Cynics might say that this was hardly a miracle given the Hebridean climate, but even in the driest of summers the basin still held water. And stranger still, the water had purifying properties. Any coin dropped into it became as shiny as new.

But the thought of tragic Mary still haunted me as we jumped off the walls of the ruin and pursued the pagan pastimes of dropping pennies into the font for good luck and stabbing our fingers into the witch's stone.

Word had it that on one day a year, the sound of the worshippers singing can still be heard by some. Dad told us that in modern times a visiting clergyman staying at a nearby bed and breakfast heard beautiful plainsong on his landlady's radio. On rushing down to ask her what she was listening to, she told him that she never turned on the radio on the Sabbath.

'You'll have heard the singing at Trumpan from the old church,' the landlady told him calmly, 'some people hear it, right enough.'

Haunting plainsong, the ghostly voices of Mary and her neighbours.

I would strain to hear it, but was not on the right wavelength. Still, it was enough to make the spine tingle all the way back to Dunvegan.

At some stage, when we were old enough to learn the truth (round about thirty-five or so), we were told that the massacre at Trumpan was, in fact, in revenge for an earlier massacre of Clanranald MacDonalds on the Island of Eigg. Maybe it was Mum who set the record straight, tired of the MacDonalds being endlessly cast as the villains. On this occasion, the chief of MacLeod went on a raid to punish the inhabitants of Eigg for a previous misdemeanour, but they had all hidden in a huge cave with a secret entrance. On the point of giving up and sailing away, a man was spotted and they were able to track his footsteps through the dusting of snow that had conveniently fallen. A fire was lit at the mouth of the cave and the trapped MacDonalds - every man, woman and child - were suffocated to death.

There was no getting round this - it was brutal. It was not the way we expected MacLeods to behave. I was not altogether comfortable with this. Dad tried to muster mitigating circumstances. It was in retaliation for a previous outrage of murder and mutilation. The chief, being a devout man had prayed for six hours in an agony of doubt before calling for the bonfire to be lit. In the end, it was up to God. If the wind stayed as it was, the smoke would not blow into the cave. If it changed direction, then it would be a sign of God's will. The wind changed direction. The MacDonalds died. And the tradition of powerful men committing mass murder, because God is on their side and speaking to them directly, is given another boost.

Mum loved Trumpan. Its position on the Waternish headland, under a huge open sky with an uninterrupted view west across the Minch to the Outer Isles, is often breath-taking. The sea can be rough and choppy, the sky glowering and the far isles hidden in mist, a forewarning of rain to come. Or the Minch can be blue and calm, the sky clear and the outlines of Harris and Lewis so sharp that the islands feel near enough to touch. Mum loved Trumpan most in the springtime, when the churchyard was thronged with daffodils shaking their yellow trumpets in the stiff westerly wind.

'I'd like to be buried here,' Mum would muse.

This was interesting, because Dad wanted to be buried at the old kirkyard in Dunvegan, in the ancestral plot. Even in death he wants to be sociable, surrounded by family. But Mum needed to commune with nature on a regular basis - or at least escape her family for a snatched half an hour. She had a fey side, in tune with things we couldn't see.

On one occasion out on Loch Dunvegan, when my parents were guests in Dame Flora's boat, Mum saw a ship in full sail. Except it wasn't a modern yacht, it was a Viking galley with blue sails. Mum was transfixed by the sight and could not understand why no one else was commenting on it. Feeling foolish, she said nothing until later. Dad said there had been no ship.

Another time, climbing the hill at the back of Suardal with Dad, she looked down on the ruins of the old house and saw a modern house beside it, gleaming in the sunshine. Yet this was before our holiday home had been built there.

But Trumpan was a long, winding drive away along single-track roads from Suardal, so chances for snatched minutes of solitude there were rare. Instead, when life got too much, she escaped to the Broch, an Iron Age fortress, a twenty minute walk from the house. She would sit atop its crumbling, beehive-shaped walls, and feel a kinship with its ghosts. No doubt its prehistoric inhabitants suffered the same trials of husbands bringing back extra mouths to feed from a foray to the neighbouring tribe, or squabbling children getting under their feet because it was raining outside.

'Where's Mum?' we would ask.

'She's gone to the Broch.'

'On her own?'

We thought it bizarre behaviour to choose to go off without any of us for company. Little did we guess that one of us - or maybe half a dozen of us - had tried her patience to the limit. We would lurk in the heather watching for her coming back. Years later, she showed us a poem she had written.

This quiet circle of fallen stone
Why does it call me again and again?
Is it because all those I have loved most dearly
Have shared its peace?
I do not know.
I have sat in the silence at all times of year,
Sparkling frost at Hogmanay
Summer sunshine and autumn gale.
The loch blue or grey, choppy or still
The castle white or drab with rain
The Tables misty or starkly black
The only sound the seabirds calling,
A dog barks or a fishing boat passes
And all is silent once more.
The familiar sweep of Cuillin to Harris hills
Never fails to bring peace.
Is it not a place of Christian good
But an older and earthier faith
Yet my troubles are eased.
No problem is solved, no worry eased
And yet I return to the daily tasks
With a measure of calm in my heart.
Someday I will be old
And will not reach my haven alone
But in my mind's eye I can return
To this quiet circle of fallen stone.

So Mum returned to her brood, unbeknown to us, with a measure of calm in her heart ready to face the next mass meal or family expedition.

* * *

There were times when Mum rebelled against the well-worn pilgrim routes to shrines of MacLeod victories and heroics, and whisked us off to MacDonald country.

Sleat, in the south of Skye, was a two hour trek away by twisting roads, beyond the bald mountain tops of the Red Cuillins. This was deep into enemy territory. A large picnic would be prepared, in case supply lines were cut. The land was inhabited by MacLeod of Dunvegan's bitterest foe and rival, MacDonald of Sleat. Warfare was no longer routine, but the odd skirmish seemed possible. We were twitchy and suspicious. Even the landscape couldn't be trusted, changing to a lush green with more trees.

But after confinement in a cramped car, stopping and starting along single track roads, we tumbled out, queasy and gulping the mild air. Armadale, our destination, was the chiefly home of MacDonald of Sleat. It lay up an over-grown, tree-lined drive. But when we got there we found the castle in ruins. In fact it was a huge anti-climax. It was not even a proper castle in our eyes. Armadale was more Victorian hotel meets the Addams Family spooky house. There was a reason for this. The MacDonalds had decamped from their fortress at Duntulm at the end of the 17th century, and this present building was a Gothic design by Georgian architect, Gillespie, commissioned by Lord MacDonald in 1815 to be an imposing chiefly residence but with all the mod-cons. He castellated the original house and added a new suite of public rooms, though a Windsor-style round tower on the plans was never realised.

We explored around it, trying to peer through gaping windows. It had a huge baronial door still intact that looked like the entrance to a fun-fair Haunted House. It was like several abandoned nineteenth century Skye mansions that we explored in the late 1960s - Waternish, Kingsburgh, Lynedale. They lay at the end of grassy driveways, sheltered by tall trees and wrapped in crinolines of rhododendron, that most favoured exotic plant of the Victorians. They stood waiting, the wind sighing through broken windows, as if vexed that the inhabitants were late back for afternoon tea.

Peering into these abandoned houses, the rooms still contained furniture, books mouldering on shelves, paper rotting on tables and curtains sagging. There was no sense that the residents had planned to leave; no bags packed, no shutters closed, no auction of possessions. So the houses waited in shabby splendour, slowly decaying.

For me, these forlorn buildings fascinated. Armadale might not have been a real castle, but it trembled with atmosphere, with Bronte-esque tragedy.

What were the last inhabitants like? Where had they gone and why had they never come back? It conjured up the ghostly house in the Walter de la Mare poem, *The Listeners*. And deep inside stirred the desire to write about tragic Victorians and bring such places back to their full splendour between the pages of a book.

I could see from the expression on Mum's face that her fantasy was much more concrete and immediate. She would rebuild Armadale with some mythical family fortune, redecorate and furnish to a high standard of taste and comfort. There would be servants, of course, and most definitely a cook. Dinner parties and dancing and walks in the grounds.

When she came out of her reverie, it was back to harsh reality. There was a swarm of squabbling children who needed somewhere to play cricket and a picnic of well-travelled egg sandwiches or corned beef.

* * *

We were veteran picnickers. We did so all over the island and in all conditions. Rain, mist, gales, heat-wave, clouds of midges - or any combination of these - have been no deterrent to MacLeod al fresco meals. They largely followed the same formula. A destination of historical interest was chosen, usually a ruin or landmark that carried some interesting or gory story attached. We would drive as near to it as we could get, and then trek the rest like a line of Sherpas carrying rugs, bats, balls, swimming towels and the holy of holies - the wicker picnic basket.

Such expeditions were often enlarged by meeting up with our Davidson-Kelly cousins (MacLeods through their mother, our lively and talkative Auntie Molly). The Kelly boys - John, Norman and Tom - were older than us and larger than life. Big, boisterous and affectionate, they were musical and funny and taught us card games like Racing Demon, which they played amid much shouting and flinging of cards off the table. They enlivened any family trip and we young ones adored them.

Our favourite spots were sandy beaches, only too rare on this volcanic island. Varcasaig, Talisker or Harlosh Island provided them. Here we could swim without slipping on seaweed-strangled rocks and cutting our feet. And, tide permitting, there could be endless games of football or cricket. The picnics themselves were timeless; a flask of tomato soup, sandwiches not given to variation, and a "chittery-bight" (usually shortbread biscuits) to sustain us after a swim.

However, modern innovation into picnic-making was bound to intrude sooner or later. It did so with startling consequences in the early 1970s. We were on a joint expedition with cousins John and Susan and their daughters, Kirsteen and Sally, to Rudha an Dunain in MacAskill country. It entailed a lengthy drive down to the Cuillins, then a long walk over rough terrain to Soay Sound and the remote stronghold of the MacAskills. With two history teachers in the party, there were many tales to tell. Once the stories had been exhausted, we repaired to the shelter of a graveyard, spread out the rugs and attacked the joint picnic with relish in the breezy sunshine.

Susan began to pour out coffee from their flask and offer it around. She turned to Dad.

'Would you like Coffee-mate?'

He gave her a slightly startled look and just a momentary pause before responding.

'Yes please.'

She reached for the powdered cream and was about to spoon it into his coffee when he yelped in protest.

'My God, what are you doing?'

Rather taken aback, Susan replied, 'Putting Coffee-mate in your coffee.' She showed him the jar of milk substitute with the trademark, Coffee-mate.

Dad roared with laughter. 'Oh, I thought you were just being familiar - calling me mate!'

It was Susan's turn to convulse with laughter. A household catch-phrase was born that day. From then on whenever he was offered coffee by Susan or John, it was, 'Coffee Mate?'

'Yes, Mate!' he'd reply with a burst of laughter.

* * *

Trotternish was another Skye peninsula that had been conquered by the MacDonalds in late medieval times and to which we would on occasion go. It was full of MacDonald places of pilgrimage, such as the grave of Jacobite heroine Flora MacDonald at Kilmuir and the ancient stronghold of Duntulm perched on a precipitous cliff top, surrounded on three sides by the sea.

Duntulm was the ancient seat of the MacDonalds of the Isles, possibly on the site of an even older fort, the Dun of David, a Viking chief. On the beach below was a long indentation in the rocks, said to be made by the keels of Viking galleys.

We were probably allowed to go there, because the MacDonalds at Duntulm were briefly cast in a good light - they saved one of our ancestors from being put to death by our own chief. During the turbulent sixteenth century, the whole of our branch of the family was being extirpated by the particularly paranoid Tormod, 12th Chief, who thought we had designs on the chiefship. They were all put to death on a single night - even a nun at remote Rodel on Harris - so he really didn't like us. Only one family member, a young boy was spared by his soft-hearted foster father. When small Norman climbed onto the knee of Finlay Morrison and put his arms about his neck, the man did not have the heart to kill him as he'd been instructed. The foster mother

Behag bribed some boatmen to take her across the Minch to Duntulm and plonked the child on the knee of Donald Gorm, Chief of the MacDonalds. The knee trick worked again, for the MacDonalds cared for the boy and he grew up with his clan. Thanks to their kindness, the Suardal branch eventually came into being.

There was, however, a more grisly baby story that was told to us, as we peered through the ruined window of Duntulm's high fortress with its dizzyingly sheer drop to the rocks and sea below. I still get butterflies thinking about it. Some poor unfortunate nursemaid was crooning to the chiefly babe in her arms, while looking out for the return of her sweetheart's boat. But she ignored the golden rule of nannies and au pairs; don't stand by an open window with a baby in your arms.

She dropped him out of the window into the raging sea. The chiefly parents never recovered. After that they left their northern castle and built one at Armadale, far away from cliffs in sheltered Sleat. I always wondered what happened to the nurse. Folklore has it that (in the days before litigation) she was put out to sea in a boat drilled with holes. No doubt a tame punishment in those days. But I hope her seafaring boyfriend was on hand to save her from such salty justice.

Ever since, I've had a fear of small children going anywhere near the edge of cliffs, open windows or sheer drops of any kind. I will rush up to complete strangers, shaking and gibbering incoherently as I point to their offspring about to launch themselves over railings into Niagara Falls or somewhere less dramatic. I believe I have saved several lives - including a MacLeod child - who was intent on clambering a fence at the zoo in his eagerness to join a grizzly bear in its enclosure.

The last time I visited Duntulm in recent years was with Dad in a wheelchair. The bumpy, undulating pathway winding through fields along the promontory, was a test both for the new wheelchair and the stamina of my children who were helping to push. At times, they ground to a halt and the uncomplaining Norman was hauled to his feet and encouraged to push his own chariot.

Duntulm was reached and the stories of babies retold once more. On the way back, however, a new legend was almost born of The Grandfather Who Was Accidentally Hurled To His Death. Back in his chariot, the bumpy return ride along the cliff top path was going well until the final part of the assault course came into view - a sharp dip to the right (and the sea) before a short steep climb to the left (and the safety of the parked car). It was at this point that we began to pick up speed. Dad was in the middle of some clan tale. The wheelchair began to freewheel to the right. Behind him, everyone - me, kids, mother-in-law - grabbed for the handles and pulled backwards to slow the momentum towards the cliff edge.

The telling of the story stopped in mid-flow, just for a second or two, as we appeared on the point of tipping the story-teller over the cliff and into the sea. Incredibly, we somehow veered to the left and conversation resumed.

Laughing that he thought his end had come, Dad needed no persuasion to climb out of his chair and push it up the bank to the car. A startled couple coming in the opposite direction gave him such looks of admiration and encouragement that they obviously thought they had witnessed a miracle - a lame old man leaping from his chair and walking unaided.

'At that speed,' they said, 'you'll win the Derby.'

* * *

Back in the days before such new-fangled transport, reaching these sites of historical interest was done on foot - at times tired and weary feet. On one occasion, our maternal grandfather came to stay. This MacDonald-supporting Robert Gorrie, was a veteran of treks through the Himalayas in his days as a forester with the India Forestry Service and so a keen explorer. A scientist and practical man, he was a recent convert to genealogy and clan history through his son-in-law, Norman. For a while he edited the Clan Donald magazine and was a keen photographer. He had the fervour of all new converts and this particular day, wanted to discover the isolated ruin of Peinduin in west Trotternish where Flora MacDonald had died and thereby pay homage to this clan heroine.

Unfortunately, the old house was not marked on his map. We set off on a long and seemingly circuitous search for Flora's last home. There was growing hunger and rebellion. Eventually, we reached a rectangular ruin.

'This is it,' Mum declared with all the bossy authority of a tour guide, plonking down the picnic rugs.

Dad's look was disbelieving, but he knew from experience a very important detail about his beloved. If Sheila didn't have meals regularly she could turn quite snippy. He said nothing.

Granddad, still at heart the gullible idealist who had enlisted for the trenches of Flanders in the First World War, believed his daughter without question. We children, sick of trudging aimlessly around the heathery moorland, couldn't have cared less.

As we picnicked by this unprepossessing oblong of stones, Granddad enthusiastically rushed about with his large camera, photographing it from every possible angle. So heady was he with the experience that he used up all his film.

Later that day, we explored further and made an embarrassing discovery. Nestling near the shore, overgrown with bracken, was the ruin of a typical eighteenth century Skye house. It was the real Peinduin. Mum, stomach full, was overcome with guilt. Granddad was crestfallen but stoical, perhaps not wanting to admit he'd been so easily taken-in by the lowly pile of stones posing as Peinduin. Dad felt bad for them both. Only later did he repeat the story out of Granddad's hearing.

'Poor Pop,' he chuckled, 'using up all his film on that ruin. It was so obviously an old sheep fank!'

Granddad though, was to get the last laugh. When staying in Edinburgh one time, en route to Skye, Bob Gorrie took his son-in-law to a MacDonald Clan dinner. Dad never really recovered from the experience. Long after he would recall the evening with a shudder.

'I had to sit through all these speeches about how great and mighty the MacDonalds were,' he spluttered. 'As if they were the most important clan of all!'

We thought this concept strange and outlandish too. MacLeods were the clan whose chiefs had stuck to the rock, with a real lived-in castle, for longer than any noble family in the land. We had glamour - a magical Fairy Flag that won battles. We had a clan society that stretched around the world like a virtual plaid binding us all together. It was obvious whose clan was the greatest. .

Only years later, when studying Scottish history at Edinburgh University did the first doubts begin to surface. The MacDonalds, it seemed, had been pretty well-known around the Western Isles. In fact, they had been Lords of the Isles for a time. Even after being defeated at the Battle of Largs in 1263, they continued to rule over large tracts of land. Indeed, there were so many of them, they needed several chiefs to organise them into various MacDonald clans. Perhaps Granddad had a point after all.

It was a bit like escaping the Moonies and going through a de-brainwashing programme. I had to accept that my earlier education may have been a fraction partisan. The MacLeods (though still glamorous and fascinating), probably did not come top in the Premier League of Most Powerful Clans throughout much of Highland history.

This already sounds like sacrilege, so I'll stop.

Orgies and Old Maid

'In Skye the Reformation was more a political than a spiritual movement. The people followed their Chiefs. They may have had some religious convictions, but what determined the issue was clan loyalty to the Chief.' So wrote, Alexander MacRae in his book, 'The Fire of God among the Heather' for the Highland Christian Literary Society in 1928.

During the seventeenth and eighteenth centuries, age-old beliefs in ghosts, witches and Fairy people were still robust and the prophecies of seers taken as seriously as any scriptures. But after the failed Jacobite Rising of 1745, the clan system was fast unravelling, the economy collapsing and the culture of the Highlands under attack with bagpipes and the wearing of tartan banned. It was a matter of time before the pious Sassenachs (Lowlanders) turned their earnest attentions to colonising the souls of the Highlanders too.

The dream of John Knox (the Scottish Reformation's leader) had been a school in every parish. This was not realised for a long time, and though local synods of the Church did set up some parochial schools, distribution was patchy.

In 1766, the parishes of Duirinish and Waternish had 2,500 "catechisable persons" and four places of worship, yet no teachers or catechists. At the beginning of the eighteenth century, the SPCK (Society for the Propagation of Christian Knowledge) had also set up schools in the Highlands to instruct pupils, with teachers using the Bible. By 1772 there were 159 such schools, but the Bibles were in English and the majority of people only spoke Gaelic. The SPCK made things a lot harder for themselves by forbidding Gaelic as a medium of instruction. It was no longer sexy; it was the language of the despised, illiterate Gael and the SPCK feared fomenting Jacobite revolt.

Here was scope for some serious missionary work. The Highland Christian Literary Society, recorded the scandalous state of affairs prevalent at the beginning of the nineteenth century in Skye.

'The island was peopled by witches, fairies and ghosts. Drunkenness and riotous excesses were associated with the most sacred events. Gatherings on the Lord's Day were fully utilized for business and pleasure. Sales and fairs were advertised at the Church door. Business was transacted as if it were a market day. On Communion occasions spirit dealers and pedlars carried on a brisk trade. On the Communion Monday, the tables were removed, the green cleared, pipers struck up their music and dancing commenced on the spot where Communion was served. So dark was the mind of the people that they saw nothing incongruous in such scenes.' ('The Fire of God among the Heather' by Alex. Macrae, 1928)

It gets worse, I'm afraid. Even the ministers were behaving badly. Roderick MacLeod, an able sportsman, violinist and favourite of the Chief, was appointed minister of Duirinish parish in 1823. Roderick not only played his violin at a ball following a funeral, but after his ordination into the ministry he had to help his co-presbyters to bed because they were so drunk.

But change was coming. In 1807, the first Gaelic Bible was published. The problem was, the people could not read their own language. Theirs was still largely an oral culture. In Duirinish in 1810, out of a population of 3,325 only about 300 could read English and none Gaelic. So a society was quickly established to open up Gaelic schools. These were not to be in competition with the parochial or SPCK schools. Their *'sole object was to teach the people to read the sacred Scriptures in their native tongue. Their work was educational, their motive was religious'* (ibid).

They were the madrasas of their day - bringing the Holy Book to ordinary people. There was no age limit; the old studied alongside the young. They 'became centres of religious awakening.' (ibid.) One of the ministers most involved in bringing the Gaelic Bible to the people was another descendent of the Suardal branch, Norman MacLeod, affectionately nick-named, Caraid nan Ghael (Friend of the Gael). He was one of a long line of Church of Scotland ministers who trace their descent from our common ancestor, Donald of Suardal.

The first half of the nineteenth century saw a wave of religious revivals in Skye. One in 1840 was started by a teacher of the Gaelic School Society, Norman MacLeod from Unish at Waternish Point. He was an old soldier who had served under Abercromby in Egypt and began to hold open air meetings at the abandoned model fishing village of Stein. When fifty boat loads turned up to hear him, he moved the place of meeting to the nearby Fairy Bridge, where three roads met and the annual fair for black cattle was held.

Then the fiddle-playing minister, Roderick MacLeod, was seized with the spirit of revival and turned from being a ridiculer of catechists to a member of the movement. It was a grassroots religious upsurge that challenged the patronage of the chiefs and landlords and their right to appoint ministers to the parishes. By 1843, this mix of evangelism and politics led to the Disruption of the Church of Scotland and the setting up of a radical Free Church.

'The greatest of all changes in the life of communities was in respect of the sanctity of the Lord's Day. In every case of a revival of religion, the people observed the day with reverence.' (ibid.)

Though even this enthusiastic chronicler did admit that in certain cases Sabbath observance might be a touch too Pharisaic. He gives the example of a bard in Harris having his bread for Sunday cut on Saturday and refusing to use plates washed on the Sabbath ever again.

Evangelical revivals seemed to have had a disproportionate effect on fiddle players. A blind fiddler, Donald Munro, from near Portree, was one of the finest players in Trotternish in the early nineteenth century. But having come under the influence of an itinerant preacher, he threw away his fiddle as an instrument of the Devil. Munro became a powerful orator and was known as the Father of Evangelical Religion in Skye. This brand of fiery Protestantism saw music, dancing, shinty and even story-telling as evils that had to be renounced if there was any chance of getting to Heaven.

Munro organised a day when his flock brought their fiddles and bagpipes to the head of Loch Snizort and set fire to the lot. The bonfire was monumental, Munro was happy, but pity the poor brides who had planned dances at their weddings that year. Weddings and funerals must have been dull affairs for some time afterwards. The minister at Duirinish in the 1840s, the Rev. Archibald Clerk, recorded in his parish review (1841) how large weddings were now a thing of the past. Before, 80 to 100 people attended and the feasting and dancing went on for at least two days. Now only five or six made up the wedding party, the fare was potatoes, herrings and a glass of whisky with no music or dancing. This may, of course, have had as much to do with the dire poverty of many Islanders, who could no longer afford mass weddings or wakes (where often so much was drunk that they 'fought fiercely amid the graves of their ancestors.') But the picture is one of a drab existence; balls and dancing parties had been given up, as had public gatherings for shinty or throwing the putting stone.

'The people live very much apart ...' (New Statistical Account of Scotland, Vol. 14. 1845)

This strain of devout but joyless religion with its strict Sabbatarianism was still going strong in twentieth century Skye. A Dunvegan woman, brought up in the Free Church, recalled the observances in her 1930s childhood.

'Everything had to be done on Saturday. Saturday was a horrid day because it was very busy, there was so much work to do - cooking, collecting water from the spring for the two days supply, (there was no mains water until 1939) cleaning the shoes - it all had to be done on Saturday.'

Another recalled, 'Sundays were deadly. You couldn't read anything but sermons, you couldn't go out in a boat ... In Glendale they wouldn't even cook on Sundays.'

In the 1960s, we Suardals gradually became aware of these restrictions, some of which we observed. Washing was never done on Sunday or hung out to dry. Not only shops and public bars, but bed and breakfasts put up their closed signs. To go for a walk was considered racy and the stricter observers thought it a sin just to sit outside in the sun. Woe betide the tourist who got stranded on the island. No Sunday newspapers, nowhere to eat out, no historical sites open, no ferries running and no escape. The purpose of the Sabbath was to go to church, eat Sunday lunch, sleep or read the Bible and go back to church again.

In one God-fearing household I visited, a large pair of binoculars was kept on the sitting-room windowsill. Maybe they were bird watchers, but I was convinced this was to keep a watchful eye on neighbours to make sure there were no signs of prodigal behaviour, such as the flaunting of washing on the line.

So church it was. The choice of kirk in Dunvegan was thus;

a) the Established Church of Scotland, with one of the highest pulpits in the land, a penitent's platform (now unused), hymn singing to a jaunty, wheezing organ and long sermons delivered in English.

b) the Free Church, with the largest congregation in the village, rousing psalm singing led by a precentor with no musical accompaniment, services in Gaelic and additional prayer meetings that could go on for an hour and a half, much of it standing.

c) the Free Presbyterian Church outside the village, gathered in a modest hut-like structure, standing for prayers and sitting for psalm-singing, where hat wearing for women was compulsory and any signs of moral decadence, such as wearing earrings or cutting their hair short, were sternly rebuked.

Sunday was a day of rest which, at the same time, demanded stamina for long kirk services. I've always been hugely admiring of my great-aunt Agnes MacLeod (sister of my grandfather Norman) who married a minister, Dugal MacLean. She was known to sit at the front of the church under the pulpit and time her husband's sermons. If she felt he had gone on long enough, she would pipe up, 'That's enough, Dugal.'

But by the '60s there were Godless forces abroad that were to undermine this social control by sermon and binoculars. The twin evils of tourism and television.

Not that the threat of outside influence was anything new. As far back as the 1840s there were sniffy remarks in the parish review that the islanders were being corrupted by contact with Lowlanders. Now tourists came from all over and wanted to come and go on the Sabbath. The move to run ferries from Kyle to Skye on Sundays was fiercely resisted. Half the population of Skye signed a petition against it. But the economic argument won.

When MacBrayne's car ferry finally chugged across the Kyle of Lochalsh that first Sunday in June 1965, it was met by a protesting group of fifty Skyemen including Big Al MacDonald from Dunvegan (the farmer who supplied our milk). A kind, mild-mannered, jovial man, Al was unswerving in his beliefs. He was also built like a MacBrayne's ferry. He lay down on the quay at Kyleakin like Canute resisting the tide of travelling cars. It took twenty-five minutes of struggle on the slipway and seven policemen to move him. Fourteen were arrested, including a minister, and charged with breach of the peace.

The Sabbatarians lost, but issued a letter of welcome to visitors reminding them that, *'An integral part of our Christian heritage is a deep respect and love for the Lord's Day. We therefore appeal to all not to desecrate God's Holy Day by travelling to and from the island on the Sabbath.'*

We never did, until in very recent years. Even now, there is a residual feeling of guilt, driving away from Skye on the Sabbath, passing Duirinish Church as quickly and quietly as possible with eyes averted, back of the neck prickling at the thought that someone, somewhere is watching the exodus through binoculars. In the '60s and '70s, such fast and loose behaviour was unthinkable.

* * *

The Television was a more invidious interloper. Transmission on Skye did not start until 1966 and then only one channel could be viewed, BBC One. The Church Synod of Glenelg summed up the dangers in its annual report on Religion and Morals of that year.

'A flood of lurid salacious matter emanates into our homes via a means which to date has resented and resisted all attempt at control and stricture. The Sabbath, for some unknown reason, seems to be the day when this medium excels in its foul moral oozings.'

One wonders how many Synod members (and on how many Sundays) had to watch enough TV on the Sabbath to draw their conclusions.

The year before, we had sat open-mouthed in amazement, as the young Church of Scotland minister in Dunvegan preached against the evils of the Television. We squirmed guiltily in our pew, as we were already deeply corrupted. At home in Durham we had imbibed *Watch with Mother* like mother's milk, lapped up endless hours of *Cracker-Jack, Top of the Pops* and *The Monkees*. We were fast-tracking to Hell.

Then the following Easter the Suardals were invited out to the Manse for tea. The minister and his young family had something exciting to show us. He led us into the sitting-room. With a flourish of a proud hand, he pointed out their new acquisition. There by the fire was a TV set. A nude picture of the Queen would not have shocked us more. As far as we knew, this was the first TV set to arrive in the village. Yet the minister did not even blush at this volte face.

We soon saw how he would prevent detection from the binoculars of the Godly. The TV had an indoor aerial. Even so, it would not take long for such scandalous news to spread around the area - not least by us blabbermouths. No doubt, it just confirmed the 'Wee Frees' in their belief that the Established Church of Scotland was hopelessly decadent and beyond all saving.

It was, however, a Church of Scotland minister preaching at Duirinish, not a firebrand of the Free Presbyterians, who brought to public attention the most debauched carryings-on ever to take place on the Sabbath in Dunvegan during this period.

He thundered from the high pulpit to the upturned faces below, of the "orgies" taking place in our midst. And these diabolical deeds were being perpetrated on the Sabbath itself. Had he uncovered some hideous cult involving human sacrifice and animals? A coven of hedonistic witches, perhaps?

No, far worse. It was tea parties at Dunvegan Castle. The heinous practice was perpetrated by none other than Dame Flora, MacLeod of MacLeod, herself.

While he gave his tirade from the pulpit, the teetotal, devout Dame Flora sat demurely and upright at the church organ which she played each Sunday, before rushing off to organise yet another orgy.

We again, were beyond saving, for all of us had participated willingly in such orgiastic get-togethers. It was one of the highlights of the week to be invited to the Castle for Sunday afternoon games and tea.

If the weather was fine, we would gather in the round Rose Garden for football. The springy, well-kept lawn was a joy to play on and we rushed about in our best kilts, shrieking instructions, no quarter given to age or ability. Dame Flora, white-haired and already in her eighties, would stand in goal, trim in her neat tartan skirt and green jacket and defend with skill.

Next came tea in the Castle dining-room, sitting around the vast table on leather upholstered chairs so big that our feet dangled high in mid-air. The portraits of former chiefs and their wives surrounded us, stern bearded men and beautiful women. The most intriguing was the 'Red Man', dressed from head to toe in a red tartan check, his head crowned in a stylish wig, his look proud. This wily eighteenth century chief chose not to risk the clan fortunes by supporting Bonnie Prince Charlie in 1745, although a Jacobite at heart. In his youth he had been involved in some skulduggery to do with enforcedly shipping off some of his own people to sell into slavery in the colonies. It was a practice indulged by the government of the day to rid themselves of bothersome criminals, but these People of the Long Ship turned out to be tenants dragged from their beds in the middle of the night, many of them women and children.

Even worse, in my eyes, he was rumoured to have imprisoned his first wife (called Janet) in the Castle dungeon until she starved to death and then took a second from among his household. Mrs MacLeod II was a dark-eyed hussy called Ann Martin whose full-length portrait hung on the wall, pouting down on us as we ate our tea with Dame Flora.

Of course, to Dame Flora, there was no such thing as a bad ancestor or a bad MacLeod, and the sins of the forefathers were briskly brushed under the flagstones. She welcomed all those who bore the name of Leod to her fortress home from around the world. She encouraged them to return. Writing her annual letters in the Clan MacLeod magazines at this time, she referred to society members as "my Clan children" and styled herself as the "welcoming Mother to the old home". She recaptured for many the essence of clanship, that paternalistic, mystical bond between chief and clan which had once existed. Like chiefs of old, she was generous with her hospitality, though in one letter, she alludes to the problems of retaining staff in these times of social upheaval.

'Heavy taxation and the insatiable demand of the tourist industry for domestic staff inevitably create serious difficulties. The warm welcome is still there, but it may be that the hospitality must be more limited and simpler than it has been.' (The MacLeod Magazine, 1967).

Unaware of such constraints, we would tuck into the tea of cucumber or salmon paste sandwiches, scones and homemade cherry cake that was a speciality of the Castle.

Later, as a student, I was a guide in this very room, eager to display my intimate knowledge of the chiefly portraits - after all I had eaten, drunk and been merry with these guys. I stood for hours as visitors filed through the room with their information cards waiting in vain for someone to ask me questions. The harder I smiled, the quicker they left the room. Finally, joy of joys, a woman approached me.

'Where is this from?' she eyed me keenly and pointed to an exhibit. It was an ashtray.

I didn't have a clue. Was this a trick question? Maybe she had sent it as a present and it represented her life savings. I began to sweat. Recovering my poise, I tried to look interested in the glass ashtray.

'I believe it's from New Zealand,' I lied. 'The Chief receives many generous gifts from kind clans people all over the world. This is one of them.'

She nodded in approval and moved on. Ann Martin looked down on me and smirked.

The only other momentous question I recall being asked (apart from where was the exit) was from another woman, this time about the curtains.

Fingering them, she said in a probing way, 'Umm, what are these drapes?'

I felt like saying, 'they're velvet and red and you pull them across at night.' Instead, I seized my chance to show off my expertise.

'They're Edwardian,' I guessed. 'Don't they set off the portraits nicely? That one there is Norman Magnus - he built the village hall. And over there is Norman, the Potato Famine Chief. He bankrupted himself to save his- '

'I like the drapes,' she interrupted and moved away with a look that said, I can read the information card for myself if I want any of that history stuff.

But back in the '60s, taking tea with a real chief, history wasn't academic. We were living it. After tea, we would run along the corridor, its walls strewn with ancient broad-swords and stags antlers, to the drawing-room for a game of cards. This was no ordinary sitting-room. Superficially, its cream-coloured walls and upholstered furniture might suggest a slightly old-fashioned modernity. A large gilded mirror hung above the stone fireplace and next to it, the portrait of Flora's younger daughter, Joan Wolrige-Gordon, looking chic and attractive in a gauzy, pastel 1920s dress.

But the casement windows revealed walls that were several feet thick and beyond the fireplace, hidden behind its venerable stone wall, we knew (with a frisson of fear) lay the dungeon. Not a spacious, echoing Hollywood dungeon, but a claustrophobic, dank-smelling, bottle-neck dungeon.

This drawing-room in which we sat at green baize card tables and played games of Old Maid or Happy Families, was the very heart of the Castle - its ancient central Keep. Here, the chiefs of old had entertained with pipers, fiddlers and bardic verse, wined and dined their guests and rivals, occasionally stabbing them to death after dinner or dispatching them to the dungeon next door.

Card games with Dame Flora might sound tame in comparison, but they were not without incident. We soon learned that the sweet-faced Dame, with her soft skin and ready smile, was not above cheating at Old Maid. The Castle party also introduced us to a viciously fast and frantic game called Pounce; a simpler version of Racing Demon where no suit had to be followed. The amount of noise, dispute and throwing about of cards that Pounce generated would have gladdened the hearts of their wilder ancestors.

No trip to a Castle tea party would be complete without a request to visit the dreaded dungeon. We would love to go and stare down its narrow hole into the dark void below, just a careless slip away. I imagined the poor Janet stuck down there in the blackness of the rock chamber while the Red Man gallivanted around in the daylight chatting up Ann Martin. This probably never happened, for the Red Man was in fact a generous man to his kith and kin, and looked after many hard-up relations as well as widows among the clan. Perhaps he was the victim of bad press from his MacDonald in-laws, but I never really trusted him.

To add to the hideousness of a prisoner's plight, there was a window half way up one of the dungeon walls - too high for them to peer through - that opened onto a secret back staircase. In olden days, food was carried up these stairs from the kitchen to the Great Hall and the smells would have wafted in to the incarcerated and driven them mad.

We knew we were safe with Dame Flora for she would never put us in such a place, even if we beat the Castle team at football. Her grandson and heir, John, was a different matter. He had visited us in Durham, sweeping in like James Bond in a sporty, open-topped car. He had told Rory and 1 that he would put us in the dungeon (probably for boring him with Beatles cards). When we scurried behind Mum and clung to her legs for protection, John had let out a peel of laughter. Then he was dashing out of our lives again on some unknown mission.

The threat was a real one. We had gasped at the story of a German friend of John's who had been lowered into the dungeon for a wager and spent a whole night down there without anyone else knowing. We spent a lot of our childhood squealing in excitement and running away from our future chief, until we realised (at about the age of forty-three) that the threat was just one of his jokes.

In the same way, John's son Hugh delighted in teasing my son Charlie, picking him up and promising to throw him in the dungeon. This in turn provoked the customary screams and laughter and repeated requests to go and look in the dungeon again. And so the tradition carries on.

Fairies, Ghosts and Donovan

Strong though the stricter Calvinist tradition remained on Skye, it never managed to completely quell the "riotous excesses" of the Gael nor eradicate much older beliefs in Second Sight or ghosts. The two traditions have bumped shoulders together down the years like brothers and rivals.

The Rev. Clark, in 1841, recorded that charms and incantations were still being used for curing diseases in cattle. Belief in silver water, Fairy arrows and charmed stones was strong and "those who could call forth their powers are held in high estimation."

Hallowe'en was still celebrated on Skye in the twentieth century, with children dressing up in fancy dress, singing songs and expecting a few pennies, an apple or orange in return. Many of the older generation born in the early years of that century (and from Free Church households) had fond memories. Mrs MacDonald from Skinidin remembered getting apples and sweets and giving oblongs of peat to the school master as fuel for the fire.

'In every house there would be coins in cream. All the children dug in to try and get the coin. There was luck in it.'

Annie MacKay and Mrs John dressed up in trousers and wore masks. The men recalled tying string to the end of cabbages and pulling them when the owners came by to give them a fright.

It was the one day in the year when food would be redistributed around the townships and not be seen as stealing - turnips being thrown in at someone's door belonging to another crofter, perhaps because they needed it more. In Colbost, the boys dug up the cabbages of a man known to be mean and gave them away. Sometimes it was just high jinks. Mrs MacDonald said that if people left anything out in their gardens, they would find them lying far away the next morning.

The tradition of first-footing at Hogmanay was strongly entrenched throughout the community too. People would visit each other's homes in the early hours of the New Year, bearing bottles of whisky or a present of food. This visiting could go on for days. To offer whisky or a bannock to the host was to give a wish or blessing to the house and ensure plenty of food for the coming year.

The first time we attempted to reach Skye for New Year was January 1962. Challengingly, it was one of the snowiest winters for decades and the advice was not to drive. Not to be denied the dream of a Suardal New Year, my parents brought the four of us (Angus was not yet on the team sheet) by train and then steamer to Portree. Torq remembers the black night being lit with flaming torches as the boat called in at Raasay to off-load supplies.

Our intrepid friend, Al MacDonald, came in a Land Rover with snow chains on its wheels to bring us across the island. It was a treacherous drive.

Mum recalled sitting up front beside Big Al with me on her knee, while Dad and the boys were having a ceilidh in the back, oblivious to the hair-raising journey through the icy, snowbound roads. Mum had her eyes closed for most of the epic run, partly because she couldn't bear to watch and partly because she was praying a lot.

We reached Dunvegan, but Suardal was cut off by snow drifts. Instead, we were taken in by the hospitable MacLeod couple, John and Morag, and their two young sons (Rory and Iain) who ran the Misty Isle Hotel. This was a luxury for all of us. Years later, I would be a waitress at the Misty, wearing a yellow MacLeod mini-kilt long after they had gone out of fashion and dealing with a range of interesting situations, such as apologising for a drunken head waitress who was loudly and liberally dousing the guests in gravy. Thankfully, that was all far in the future.

There is one episode that has stuck in my mind from that winter adventure of '62. On January the eighth we set out to spend the day at Suardal, walking the three miles with Rory and I being pulled on a sledge for much of the way. It was my fourth birthday. It is not the beauty of snow-covered MacLeod's Tables or ice-bound loch that I remember, but arriving at the start of the Suardal track and being turfed off the sledge, our transport now useless in the virgin snow.

'Follow me and put your feet in my footsteps,' Dad instructed, in a rather wise patriarchal way.

I was doing just that, when all of a sudden I was plunged into a snow hole and disappeared from view. Admittedly, it doesn't take a huge snow drift to envelop a four year-old, but it was disconcerting nevertheless. Deep, powdery snow, big tiring strides, concentration on the footprints. Then an instant later, down into a cold white cell, the world muffled, arms reaching in to haul me out.

The flip-side to this cold alarming memory, was full of bright warmth. I was sitting up high, a long way from the ground, in an armchair at Suardal. Beside me a fire was blazing and the room was full of brilliant light, presumably from the dazzling snow that marooned us beyond the large windows. I was presented with a doll. We sat in the chair together, tingling as the fire warmed. Happy Birthday.

There was a scene in the film, *Dr Zhivago*, where Omar Sharif arrived on a troika through the snow to his boarded up summer house, deep in the countryside. Whenever I see it, it transports me back to the first birthday of which I have conscious memory; of travelling by sledge, of falling down a footprint into a snow drift and arriving in a world of fire and light.

* * *

As we grew older, Hogmanays on Skye became more frequent. There were times when we younger members were left in Edinburgh with grandparents while the older ones made the journey. But one year, we younger three were invited with our parents to spend New Year at the Castle. It was a magical experience, each with our own room in the south wing, from where we could hear the waterfall, Rory Mor's Lullaby, that had lulled the seventeenth century chief to sleep. Each night, meals would be hauled up on the noisy, creaking 'dumb waiter' from the kitchens below to the dining-room and we would be allowed to eat with the grown-ups.

Dame Flora's eldest daughter, Alice MacNab was there with her husband Archie, the 22nd Chief of the MacNabs and a veteran of the Raj in India who fascinated us with the gadgets he produced from his pockets. He seemed to carry about him a canteen of miniature implements; knives, scissors, string, no doubt everything he would possibly need to survive a long train journey across the Sub Continent or the siege of Lucknow.

Archie was old, white-bearded, out-spoken and rather crotchety and we could have watched and listened to him for hours. He indulged us and talked to us as if we were adults. When he heard I had just started at a convent school, he fixed me with a blazing look as if I was embarking on a life of subversion.

'Don't become a nun,' he barked, 'it's a dog's life!'

So startled was I by this revelation that it's the one piece of adult advice I've consistently heeded.

There were other guests that came and went, enjoying the hospitality. After dinner, we sometimes played charades or a Castle game called 'The Tin Game.' This was a sophisticated version of Blind Man's Buff. Tin cans filled with pebbles or rice would be hidden around the room. Two blindfolded contestants would be set against each other, attempting to find and collect as many tin cans as they could and store them somewhere safe from their rival. Everyone else watched and shouted encouragement.

My finest moment came, when hearing my opponent (Rory) scuttling past me with a tell-tale rattle of cans, I dived to stop him.

'Well tackled!' cried Jumbo Wakefield, a former England international rugby player. I may not have won the game, but I felt I had passed selection.

By day, we played hide and seek in the frosty gardens and by night joined the adult world of after dinner chat in the Fairy Room, a small cosy chamber in Alasdair Crotach's sixteenth century tower where a baby chieftain had been rocked to sleep by his Fairy mother, wrapped in the Fairy flag. When we retired to bed, the chilly sheets would be warmed by an old-fashioned china 'pig' - a Victorian version of the hot water bottle - which had appeared in our absence as if by Fairy magic.

Within a few short years, we were coming regularly to Skye for New Year and allowed to take part in the ancient tradition of First Footing. At times this was just a late-night version of regular visiting, sitting around growing slightly bored with an empty glass of lemonade while the grown-ups talked ad nauseam. But it had its diverting moments. First Footing for

Beginners was being taken to Cathy and Charlie Heron's at Rose Cottage where Cathy, with her quick laugh, would fill us full of rich Dundee cake and Charlie chatted about football to my brothers. The highlight was turning on the TV to watch the White Heather Club with Andy Stewart singing and dancing their way into the New Year.

Intermediate First Footing meant we visited as far as the near end of the village. One time, in the lively household of Angie Plum (Angus MacDonald the Plumber), the room was full of people talking loudly, singing, drinking and laughing. A youth called John got up and, weaving in a leisurely fashion, made his way towards the sitting-room door. Just at this point, someone arrived and the door swung open, pinning the unsuspecting John to the wall. We watched with breath held to see if he would burst out of this sudden imprisonment or be discovered squashed flat like a cartoon mouse. The door remained open for quite some time while the new visitors came and others went in search of refreshment.

Finally, someone closed the door again. John emerged, not a flicker of surprise or protest on his face and continued to negotiate his way out of the room as if nothing had delayed him.

First Footing was not a one-way system. We might First Foot on Hogmanay while others would visit us on subsequent nights. One year, three villagers led by Rory of the Misty appeared like The Three Musketeers, full of bonhomie and whisky. They sat by the fire, producing bottles from their pockets and liberally offering drams around. They stayed for quite some time.

At one point, Donald Angus, who had grown-up in a house on the pier, cried mysteriously but with obvious satisfaction, 'We're all big boys!'

Eventually they drove off into the night. Late the next evening, just as we were making for bed, headlights appeared over the brow of the hill. In trooped the same three Highlanders.

'We're all big boys, Norman!' cried Donald Angus while Rory of the Misty poured out deep drams and they all sat down once more, presumably oblivious to the fact that they had been out the night before.

* * *

The "riotous excesses" of drinking, music and story-telling that so upset the nineteenth century missionaries and that a century and a half of evangelising had not quashed, were not confined to Hogmanay. Ceilidhs, those informal get-togethers in each other's homes where each took a turn in entertaining the others, were some of the highlights of our holidays.

We loved it when our parents invited out friends and neighbours to the house for a ceilidh. The sitting-room furniture would be pushed back against the walls and mattresses brought in for extra seating. Dad would go down to the Misty to get in liquid supplies and we would practise our party pieces -

songs, recorder pieces (Don was particularly adept at playing through his nose) or corny jokes. Our cousins John and Norman could play the bagpipes, cousin Tom the fiddle. John once stole the show with some performance art. Half way through the ceilidh he disappeared for a while, returning with half his beard shaved off. By the end of the ceilidh, he was completely clean shaven.

There was a group of young teachers from Liverpool who camped each summer at the village campsite (even bravely at New Year on one occasion). Dave entertained us with his guitar and a string of songs, from Liverpool folk to Woody Guthrie that became firm family favourites. Sometimes, John the chieftain, would come and sing songs in Gaelic or German. The only person who refused to set foot inside Suardal, was our nearest neighbour. It was nothing personal. It was the pre-fabricated house to which he took exception because it had been built on the Sabbath. So keen were the southern labourers to escape the rural delights of Skye that they had built the house in a week, carrying on over the weekend to get it finished. Our neighbour did, however, allow his family to visit.

One particular ceilidh was more eventful than most. Some MacLeods from across the loch had been brought by our friend, Peter MacAskill. One of them was in belligerent mood and Peter obviously felt responsible for his conduct. This MacLeod, having mouthed off a bit while others were performing, decided he needed to answer the call of nature. He headed off to find relief.

There were two such places in the house for the divesting of quantities of drink - a cloakroom to the left, or a bathroom up the passage to the right. The etiquette of the day was that women tended to use the right-hand option next to the bedrooms while the men used the cloakroom. It was a general guide and not something to declare clan warfare over - until this particular night.

MacAskill, already unnerved by his friend behaving badly, saw him making for the bedrooms in open defiance of house policy and suspected havoc. MacAskill dived after MacLeod. The ceilidh continued, somewhat falteringly. There followed the sound of muffled shouting and thuds.

Members of the home team pursued the source of the noise to find Peter struggling on the floor with MacLeod. MacLeod had taken a wrong turning into a bedroom and, before he could rectify his mistake, MacAskill had pounced.

'Get out of here!'

'I just want a -'

'You've insulted the Suardals.'

'I just need a - ugh!'

Soon this fringe event was drawing the crowds. Historically, MacAskills were vassals of the MacLeods, the rowers of their longboats, important but subordinate. At the sight of Peter pinning his friend to the ground, another of his clan, Willie MacAskill, cried with glee, 'It's good to see the MacAskills on top of the MacLeods for once!'

It could have been the touch-paper to revolution. Instead, the shaken MacLeod was rescued and allowed to complete his mission and the rest of the evening went with a swing. There was much piping and story-telling into the early hours, just as our ancestors would have enjoyed.

Peter, a local entrepreneur, was a great host of ceilidhs himself. With his wife, he had renovated an old 'black' house at Colbost across the loch, as well as a former illicit whisky still and opened a tea room called the Three Chimneys. They gave atmospheric ceilidhs in the peat-reeking, low-ceilinged house, around the open fire. An old-fashioned 'box' bed stood in the shadows and was used by a local couple on their honeymoon night after one such ceilidh.

Peter was constantly having run-ins with the Free Presbyterians in his native Glendale over his attitude to Sunday openings and enthusiasm for licensed premises. So it was with great amusement that he recounted the following tale.

He was attending the funeral in Glendale of a much respected Free Presbyterian elder, for whom not only the whole community had turned out, but several important ministers from all over the Highlands. Outside the church, the local minister (with whom Peter had had several clashes over Sunday opening) came over and shook his hand to show that there was no bad feeling towards him personally.

To Peter's consternation, this triggered a stampede towards him of the other ministers - "a gaggle of about six!" - who all solemnly shook his hand, obviously taking him to be some budding young elder or local worthy. Behind him stood all his relations and staunch FPs who would have been thrilled to shake the hands of these men.

'It was like being greeted by the Queen or Superstars,' Peter recounted with a chuckle. 'My relations' eyes were popping out on stalks!'

* * *

Dad was the best of story-tellers and his favourite ceilidh piece was to tell of how our ancestor, Donald of Suardal, single-handedly defended Dunvegan from being sacked by a renegade ship of the infant American Navy. John Paul Jones, a Scot from Kirkcudbright and a captain in the US Navy, was roving around the coast of Britain during the War of Independence, behaving like a pirate and generally causing mayhem in the shipping lanes. At the end of August, 1779, he appeared off Skye in an old 42-gun French East Indiaman, *Bon Homme Richard*, which he named in honour of Benjamin Franklin and his *Poor Richard's Almanack*.

Sailing into Loch Dunvegan, intent on attacking the Castle, Jones forced on board a local fisherman to guide him up the loch. The clansman, knowing the chief was away from home, (ironically on military service in America) realised the extent of the danger and feared the worst. At the same time, there was consternation at the Castle where the ship had been spotted and the factor was organising the removal of all the plate and valuables.

Then movement was spotted along the lochside. To Jones's dismay, he saw men carrying some heavy object with scores of clansmen following along behind. What was going on? he asked the local guide.

'That is the clan gathering for battle,' replied the quick-witted man. Obviously they were carrying a cannon to defend the Castle.

At the sight of such resistance, John Paul Jones retreated and sailed off to cause havoc elsewhere. What the local man had not told him was that the long procession of people were not rallying to fight, but making their way to a funeral. The heavy object being carried was no cannon, but a coffin. The whole community had turned out to mourn the popular and respected Donald of Suardal who was being carried to his last resting place, the old burial ground of Kilmuir.

And so, Dad would always conclude with pride and satisfaction, Donald MacLeod, tacksman of Suardal and armourer to the clan, served his chief as faithfully in death as he did in life. I think a pat on the back for the quick-thinking fisherman is also deserved.

* * *

A belief in ghosts and witches also clung on into recent times. As late as 1880, an Elder of the Free Kirk in Uig, brought a charge of witchcraft against a local woman and her five daughters, accusing them of using their wicked powers to steal milk from their neighbours' cows. The local law officer was more sceptical and no one was burned at the stake as they would once have been.

Ghost stories were still recounted when we were children, though sometimes with a hushed, embarrassed air as if they should not really be believed. A local man, Lachy, told me of his sister-in-law who, after marrying and moving into her new home, had seen the ghost of a woman dressed in green. Lachy knew from his parents that the green lady had lived there before the First World War. Lachy's sister-in-law called on the assistance of her father, a retired minister from Waternish called MacArthur. He too heard strange banging and saw locked doors opening and prayed for her to go, but the restless ghost would not leave. Then after the Second World War she disappeared.

We revelled in any ghost stories, especially ones associated with tragic happenings. One was told by Joan Wolrige Gordon. On a spring night in 1961, she was in the Castle drawing-room with a group of friends listening to My Fair Lady on the gramophone. Suddenly, one of the friends, Monica Baldwin (a former nun) went pale with shock and excused herself from the merriment. Afterwards, in a letter, she described what she had seen with her 'inside eyes'.

A bearded, sandy-haired man with a bloodied smashed jaw and light blue eyes blazing with fury, was being thrown down the hole in the dungeon roof.

'I was very keenly aware of his immense vigour,' Monica wrote to Joan, 'and the fact that he was breathing hard, panting like an animal hot from the fight. In fact the fury of the fight was still in him ... Nobody spoke; there was just the shuffling round of the men who were stuffing him into the dungeon and his own very loud and rather dreadful panting with rage and pain.'

Eight years later, a complete stranger wrote to Joan about a disturbing experience on visiting the Castle that kept haunting her in dreams. Walking up the sea gate steps she had an overwhelming feeling of unease and hopelessness.

'I remember,' wrote Antonia MacLean, 'looking back at the two flat-top mountains and wanting to stop. The whole visible world had become sinister.'

Subsequently, she kept dreaming she was a kilted young man with long reddish hair being hauled up the steps before being imprisoned or killed. Joan speculated with Dad as to what the two women might have experienced. Dad was convinced that Monica Baldwin had witnessed the capture of the sixteenth century Donald Breac, guardian to his young nephew Chief Norman, who was still a youth. Both Donald Breac and the young chief were victims of Wicked Iain Dubh, a usurper from the same family branch who was ruthlessly wiping out all opposition to his taking over as chief. Arriving through the sea gate after the funeral of the late chief, John of Waternish, the chiefly family were trapped and murdered. Dad believed Antonia MacLean had seen the young chief Norman climbing the sea-gate steps to his death, while Monica's vision had been of his furious uncle, tricked by his own brother Iain and unable to protect his young charge. He emanated an anger so strong it was felt four centuries later.

Apparently when renovation work was going on at the Castle in the '60s, there were all sorts of strange incidents experienced - bad feelings, walls of ice-cold air - stirred up amid the old walls. One guest was even terrified by the rattling of chains. All was explained in the morning. The steamboat had come in and anchored off the nearby pier, jangling its chain as it dropped anchor.

Suardal, we were thrilled to hear was not without its own ghost. Mum, on more than one occasion had felt the presence of a female spirit standing with her in the kitchen, telling her to be calm and that all would be well. Both she and Dad believed it to be the eighteenth century ghost of Ann Campbell, wife of Donald of Suardal, and mistress of the old house paying a visit to the new. Like Mum, Ann Campbell had a large family and no doubt an extended township around her of friends and dependents for whom to cater. She must have recognised a woman under pressure.

Mum was not the only one to sense the Lady of Suardal's presence. Ann Cunningham, an Aberdonian student who came to help out at Suardal when we were small, also felt her there. As did cousin Susan, another practical, level-headed woman. None of them were given to flights of fancy; that was much more the preserve of their menfolk. What the ghost's presence demonstrated, of course, was the pressing need for calm in a household of boisterous, noisy, warring MacLeods. This ghost might have sounded a bit too tame and domesticated for our liking, but a ghost was a ghost, and we happily laid claim to her.

Student Ann had her own experience of premonition before the very first time she came to us in 1960. She had a dream of a very small girl sitting on a blue sofa and quite determinedly saying, 'No!'

At this point she should clearly have called off the whole arrangement because it was undoubtedly a warning. (She was later to be given the honorary title of Suardal Serf for all the depraved behaviour she had to endure, such as our enthusiasm for drinking the bath water. She was only saved by marrying Bill Watson, a handsome Fife farmer with a thatch of blond hair and an accent as thick as corn stocks whom we all instantly took to our hearts. The Serf won her freedom but Bill was indentured as Suardal Stonemason). Brave Ann came and before long, witnessed a young Janet sitting tight to the blue sofa in Suardal repeating her favourite word. Apparently, I said 'no' so often that I was nick-named 'Niet' after the Russian foreign minister of the time, Krushchev, who was saying no a lot to the Americans.

But in sweeter moments, dressed in my white nightie ready for bed, I was named the Suardal Fairy. Because, while it was possible to be sceptical about witches or even ghosts, we obviously all believed in Fairies.

* * *

Incidents of Second Sight, either premonitions about things to come, or the seeing of things that have already happened, were widely reported in Skye before the religious Rivivals of the nineteenth century. Dr Johnson, on his famous trip to the island in 1773 was intrigued by many stories of Second Sight. One was of the innkeeper at the 'change-house' in Dunvegan "seeing" his customer, Lt. Keith, dead in his chair three hours before it actually happened. One wonders why, harnessed with such knowledge, the innkeeper didn't call 'time' a little sooner. Often incidents were told of strange lights or fires being seen in places before a death occurred there, or the sound of banging like nails in a coffin.

Derek Cooper, in his book Skye, recalls talking to a Portree man in the 1960s about his Victorian grandmother who made shrouds for the local undertaker. John MacKenzie's grandmother could sometimes be heard busy at her sewing machine the night before a sudden death - unexpected to everyone but herself.

A local man, Iain Stewart of Greep, was also credited with Second Sight. He used to see funerals before they happened, dragging people off the road because a procession was going past. He would say who the mourners were but never who had died. Iain would walk the moors to avoid going by roads in case he saw things. It is said, Iain once saw a cafe full of soldiers. Later, during the First World War, he walked into that very cafe in Paris.

Skye historian and story-teller, Otta Swire, records that the inhabitants of remote St Kilda (part of MacLeod territory) often knew of world events before any ships called with news. They had foreseen the outbreak of the First World War in 1914 and also the death of Queen Victoria. The first ship that put in to the island after her death found the islanders already in mourning. 'The Seer saw it,' they replied.

It was also believed that the only time the cuckoo was heard in St Kilda was when a MacLeod of MacLeod had died.

I believe I had a latter day experience of this. One holiday at Suardal in the late summer of 1977, I was woken by an urgent banging on the window. When I drew back the curtain to investigate, I was startled by a gigantic crow flapping at the windowpane. It was quite a shock and most unusual. Knowing of the cuckoo story we speculated as to its meaning. Dame Flora had died at the end of 1976. Surely nothing had happened to her successor, John? Later that day news came that Joan, Dame Flora's daughter and mother of Chief John had died.

Alexander MacKenzie in his book 'The Prophecies of the Brahan Seer', published in 1877, speculated about the origins of this Highland phenomena.

'It is thought that the Second Sight in Scotland may have originated in a late Stone Age priesthood associated with ancestor worship, which was used as a means of keeping in touch with the spirits who inhabited the stone circles and burial mounds and who were later to be called fairies.'

To some, Second Sight was therefore a gift of the fairies, or of ancestors. My parents were Highland enough to believe in such powers. So they would not have been unnerved by the following story of premonition.

When Mum was in hospital losing her battle with cancer, a friend from New Zealand, Liz Pindar, turned up without warning. We knew she was over here travelling, but she turned up earlier than expected. Liz had had a dream in which Sheila was standing on a long beach looking out to sea and Liz felt she had to get in touch. I took her with the children to see Mum. Amy played her recorder while Liz sang *Over the Sea to Skye* and Charlie played around his grandmother's chair. The next day, sooner than the doctors had predicted, Mum died.

Nearly six years later, Liz rang up early one Sunday morning quite out of the blue. A feeling had been building all week that she had to get in touch. She had no idea that Dad was recovering in hospital from a gastric illness. About half an hour later, the hospital rang to say Dad had taken a sudden turn for the worse. By the time we got to hospital he had died of a blood clot to the lung.

Speaking to Liz later that day, she told us that she had had the same dream again about Sheila on the beach. Except this time, standing further down the same beach, was Norman. Liz, it would appear, had the gift of the fairies.

* * *

A Stone Age priesthood. It turned out that this was not completely a thing of the past either. There were strange and exciting goings-on in the neighbouring peninsular of Waternish in the 1960s that sounded similar. To our delight, the folk singer, Donovan, the nearest we British had to Bob Dylan, moved to Skye. He bought a clutch of houses in the village of Stein - including the old schoolhouse by the shore - and also the deserted island of Isay (meaning ice-isle) about a mile and a half away in Loch Bay, which Samuel Johnson had once joked about buying. With Donovan came a ready-made commune of hippies, ready to live off the land and be creative.

We spent several holidays trying to spot Donovan, but he was more elusive than the Golden Eagle. Occasionally, after trips to Trumpan, we would call in at the Stein Inn, a dark smuggler of a bar. It had stone walls, small windows and a tiny black wooden booth like a Punch and Judy stall from which drinks were served. Children were not allowed in this intimate front bar with its shelves of bottles. So imagine our excitement on meeting some of Donovan's followers sitting in the back room drinking.

They were satisfactorily hairy and spoke with perky Cockney accents. Dad wanted to know what plans they had for Eilean Isay. We had landed once on this small island from the chief's launch and found a substantial ruined house with a flight of steps. It had a grisly history. Here, Roderick MacLeod of Lewis had laid on a banquet for two branches of his own family, and afterwards stabbed them to death, one by one. Isay had been well populated and in the 1840s still had 15 families living "in considerable comfort" because of its great fertility, according to the Rev. Clark. But the last twelve crofting families had been removed in 1860 and replaced by sheep.

Were Donovan's friends going to till the land and make it fertile once more? Perhaps they were going to rebuild the house? Dad was keen to tell them of its history and of how, in 1773, Dr Johnson had been offered the island by the chief and was highly pleased to be given the title of Isay.

One of the hippies, with a name like Chips or Flick, nodded as if this all made perfect sense.

'So what are you going to do on Isay?' Dad asked.

'We're going to build pyramids and obelisks,' replied Chips with enthusiasm.

We gawped at him in wonderment. This sounded seriously whacko. Dad's face was a picture of suppressed consternation. He drew fiercely on his Woodbine cigarette. But he did not pour cold water on their ambitions.

Afterwards he laughed and said, 'It'll never happen.'

Some did settle in the area and raise families. We would see them occasionally at bazaars in the village hall, bare-foot and swishing about in hippy skirts with small winsome children at their heels. Once, we saw the man himself, whizzing by in his Land Rover, curly mop of hair unmistakeable. Donovan. Mellow-Yellow. A blur of a face behind a wheel. A giddy, hippy, hedonistic moment - then it was over.

Better than all this, was the time we almost experienced nirvana. One afternoon, Dad returned from a walk and, with breath-taking nonchalance, announced that Donovan's Land Rover had gone by with John Lennon sitting beside him.

'John Lennon?' we shrieked. 'John *Lennon!*'

Yes, he was pretty sure it was John Lennon. Rory and I rushed out of the house and raced down the track in pursuit of our hero. Of course, by the time we got there, they were long gone. But we hung about for an age, just in case they should return. Was it really John? The thought was mind-exploding, more fantastical than a thousand pyramids on Island Isay. John Lennon had not only been on Skye, but passed the bottom of our track. We could almost sense it in the air, in the settled dust after the swoosh of tyres, in the empty space where moments before they must have been.

Donovan and John Lennon. It had never occurred to me that pop stars could be friends with each other, go on holiday together or drive down a remote road in a simple Land Rover like lesser mortals, probably singing each other's songs.

We never saw them, but like true followers we believed. A legend had passed the end of our lane. We had been that close. I wonder if John had glanced out of the window at the tousled-haired Highlander that was my father and thought fleetingly, 'Hey, that fella looks a bit like Ringo.'

Donovan did not stay on Skye. He sold on and disappeared to the deserts of New Mexico like a biblical hermit in search of even remoter (though warmer and drier) communion with nature. The followers melted away. Dad was right - the obelisks never got built. Eilean Isay is still populated by sheep and awaiting its renaissance.

* * *

The end of the holiday would always come too quickly. We would be roused early for the long journey back to Edinburgh and, yawning, watch our parents load up the car, often plagued by a swarm of midges in the still morning air. It was a boring, restless period that seemed to go on for an age while Dad found extra tasks to do or was overcome with the sudden desire to sit down and write his holiday postcards. Mum would steer him back on track by reminding him how far we had to go.

'A prayer!' he would shout, delaying us further.

We'd gather round while Mum gave an extempory prayer of thanks for our time at this beautiful place and asking for a safe journey. Then we would be walking off down the track, following the overloaded car, glancing back wistfully at the shuttered house and the stone ruin. At this final moment, Dad would disappear again.

'Where is he now?' Mum would sigh, car engine running. 'It's like trying to scrape a barnacle off a rock.'

The recalcitrant 'barnacle' would be found in the ruins of old Suardal communing with his ancestors, maybe summoning up strength for the busy term ahead.

'Come on Dad, Mum's waiting!'

In later years, when John and Susan had a house on Skye, our cousin would come over early and play us away on his bagpipes. Or if his family left the island first, Rory would be taken over to Roag to play them a tune of farewell. John's piping helped Mum to scrape the barnacle from the Suardal rock, for Dad had to leave while his nephew was still playing.

So it was that Dad, to the strains of *My Home* or *Mist Covered Mountains*, would stride kilted from the family homestead like many of his ancestors must have done before him, and, with deep reluctance, take the road south.

Zizz Zizz Zizz and The Germans

There were rare and exciting summer holidays when Mum persuaded Dad to go abroad instead of to Skye. These were always camping trips; the cheapest option for a family of seven on a schoolmaster's pay.

In preparation, there would be a dummy run of erecting tents in the school grounds - an old orange ridge tent and a new-fangled frame one with interlocking poles guaranteed to nip fingers and that required a knowledge of advanced engineering to put together. This stood us in good stead until one year it was left overnight on the school playing field for its weather-proofing to dry and was pinched never to be recovered.

In the '60s, these expeditions were exclusively to France. Mum had a French friend, Marie-Therese Le Prince, whose family home was in Normandy and Dad had been to France on a school trip in the 1930s and fallen in love with the whole package - history, countryside, food and songs. The French had been instrumental in his courtship of Sheila Gorrie. Her French exchange friend, Marie-Therese, had needed a partner for a dance in Edinburgh. Sheila's boyfriend at the time asked Norman to make up a foursome. Bad decision. Norman and Sheila quickly fell in love.

They honeymooned in Paris while Marie-Therese went on to marry a jovial French count called Philippe de Maton. By bizarre coincidence, it turned out that during the Second World War, Philippe was one of the gunners who had fired on Dad's ship *The Glengyle* in Oran, during the North Africa landings. (Philippe was a member of the Foreign Legion which was then still fighting for the French Vichy Government against the Allies).

Whenever they met, they would roar with laughter about it. Philippe maintained that they were deliberately aiming not to hit. Dad, whose ship was straddled by bombs and whose neighbouring vessel was hit and the first mate killed, said, 'It didn't seem that way to the British matelot!'

We would camp in the grounds of Lamberville chateau, where Marie-Therese grew up and where her mother still lived. This was less than twenty years after the end of the Second World War and they still talked of the Occupation, how when the Germans moved into their home, one of the family portraits had dropped and split in two as if guillotined. They had been occupied in turn by Germans, British and American soldiers. The Germans had been the best behaved (though the Le Princes had refused to speak to them at meals) and the Americans the worst, leaving the house in a mess.

It was in this cool, shadowy house that I had my only fey experience. One night I dreamt of a smiling moustachioed man beckoning me upstairs into a room at the end of the corridor. When I later asked about the room I was told it had been the study of the late Monsieur Le Prince and was shown his photograph. It was the man in my dream.

The first time we visited, I had contracted mumps from my brothers and spent a week lying with swollen jaw in the orange tent unable to eat, listening to the others playing among the trees. Dad tried to relieve the misery with a startling trick with his false teeth. He dropped them out of his mouth, grimacing hideously, then put them in a pocket. Moments later, he reached into a sponge bag, flourished a blue plastic soap box and before my mesmerised eyes, whipped off the top to reveal his teeth and popped them back in his mouth. I was hugely impressed and clamoured for more false teeth magic. It was years before I realised he had a spare set.

To us, the Le Princes and de Matons were exotic. Among their many relations was a monk dressed in a white habit and teenage girls who danced rock'n'roll in wide summer skirts and didn't know how to twist. There were long meals of many courses and much jabbering in French which Mum worked hard to translate. Dad would gesticulate a lot and speak in his Maurice Chevalier accent which seemed to delight them enormously.

One year, in an attempt to avoid the tortuous drive south to the ferry, my parents discovered an overnight train service on which cars were carried. The only problem was, that to embark on such a wonder train, entailed a four-hour drive northwards to Stirling in Scotland. They endured much teasing from friends. 'Stirling,' they crowed, 'the gateway to the Continent!'

In the summer of '64, at Granddad's instigation, there was a mass family holiday in Brittany of MacLeods and Gorries. Each family rented a cottage around a courtyard and met up for communal evening meals in the biggest house, which was ours. There were shared expeditions and frequent trips to the beach. Sunburn, rock-hard bolsters for pillows and burying a grinning Granddad in the sand. Games of cricket that brought curious French children to watch. Football.

One day, Rory's football went sailing off along the crowded beach. A determined seven year-old, he went in pursuit. Finding what looked like his ball among a gaggle of French children, he picked it up. They gawped at him in astonishment and protested - probably along the lines of, 'Hoy, what you doing with our ball?'

Rory said something in reply and returned triumphantly with the ball tucked beneath his arm.

'What did you say to them?' Mum asked curious.

With a nonchalant shrug, Rory answered, 'I said zizz-zizz-zizz, just like they do.'

There were times on our camping holidays when things didn't go so smoothly. Once the zip of the orange tent broke in the middle of a gale and the tent was only prevented from flying to Russia by the frozen bodies anchoring it to the ground. Another particularly wet and windy night saw us abandon camp above the white cliffs of Dover and check into a bed and breakfast. We caused notoriety the next morning by eating all the diabetic marmalade belonging to another guest and Dad had to scour the south of England for a replacement jar.

To Torq these holidays were a particular hell. For one, he was with his family, and two, it was always during the cricket season. He spent these periods of exile from BBC radio in quests for British newspapers that would give him the latest test scores.

There was one memorable low point in Rouen in the rain, when for some now forgotten reason, Dad was leading us through the town wearing a mac over his kilt. To the inhabitants of Rouen it was obviously a deranged trouserless man with a straggle of wet kids messily eating ice-cream. It was too much for Torq. He crossed the street in the hopes no one would think him in anyway related and went in search of *The Daily Telegraph.*

He was never happier than when spinning a cardboard wheel of complicated cricketing calculus, playing his own fantasy matches and writing down the scores. Summer holidays were punctuated with the sound of Torq's happy humming and spinning, in contented moments when he could escape into the ordered world of cricket.

* * *

The Second World War was a constant reference point to the adults in our lives. Sentences would frequently begin, 'Before the War ...' or 'After the War ...' as if it was some latter-day watershed akin to BC and AD.

Granddad had fought in the trenches in the First World War and had nightmares years afterwards. Mum was told by Granny never to ask him about it. The only time he spoke about it to us was when showing photos of his admired elder brother, Peter, who had survived the first conflict only to be killed on board a hospital ship in the next. Naively I asked, 'Did he think he would live through the Second because he lived through the First?'

Granddad answered, 'I suppose he did.'

My grandparents had holidayed in Germany in the 1930s, but their reaction to Chamberlain's peace treaty with Hitler in 1938 was contrasting, according to Mum. Granddad was palpably relieved that war had been averted, while Granny was ashamed, especially when the Nazis moved swiftly to occupy Czechoslovakia.

I remember Granny saying in a voice full of regret, 'I can't really forgive the Germans - not after two wars.'

I never heard Mum speak against them. She had even learnt German at school. But Dad turned tight-lipped and twitchy when Germans were mentioned (unless it was the heavyweight boxer, Max Schmeling). In the navy during the war, he had been in the thick of it; from the evacuation of Crete to the Arctic convoys to Russia. But he played down the danger, preferring to talk of the comradeship below deck, the lively runs ashore, the blessed moments of tranquillity on leave with his mother and aunt, reading Jane Austin aloud. But we were aware of his frostiness towards Germans in sharp contrast to his effusive praise of all things French. It chimed with the pervasive culture of boys' comics and war films that portrayed plucky Brits versus stiff Germans in ubiquitous Nazi uniforms speaking in robotic pidgin English. Apart from the occasional conversation about maybe one day going to the Passion Play in Oberammergau, Dad resisted the idea of holidaying anywhere German-speaking.

Once on a French campsite, Dad began to pace and twitch. It soon became apparent that we had pitched up next to a German family. When our ball rolled in front of their tent we went cautiously and full of curiosity to retrieve it. The man smiled - he was shaving out of doors like our own dad loved to do - and tried to talk to us before giving back our ball. He didn't appear the least bit scary, we reported back.

Finally, with deep breaths and encouragement from Mum, Dad plucked up the courage to speak to our neighbour. They could understand little of what the other said, but enough to know that they had both been in the navy.

'He was bound to be alright,' Dad said, 'he was a matelot.'

Dad might have baulked at going to Germany, but he couldn't stop the Germans coming to him. And so the day came, one summer on Skye, when two tall, handsome students appeared up the Suardal track and asked if they could pitch their tent and beg some water. With Dad out somewhere, Mum agreed at once and let them put their tiny tent on the hallowed ground of the Suardal football pitch. This had never happened before. There was a grassy patch half way down the track, out of sight of the house where people had been allowed to camp before, but this was right in the middle of the view of the loch from the picture windows. When Dad returned, we told him with some glee that they were German and Mum had allowed it. Through the evening Dad grew tight-lipped and twitchy. The young men bedded down beneath the sunset, their long legs sticking out of their undersized tent. Dad kept glancing over. We kept watching Dad. Finally he could bear it no longer. He strode out to the tent. Would they like to come in for a dram?

They turned out to be medical students from Bavaria. They were amusing and friendly, liked whisky and all things Scottish. Most of all, they were bafflingly attentive and eager to listen to Dad's tales of the clan. They couldn't hear enough of them. As Dad appeared to be going through the entire repertoire, the rest of us went to bed and left them to it.

In the morning the whisky was finished and the long-legged students took a while to pack-up. Dad invited them in for breakfast and they were treated to the full works; porridge, oatcakes, readings and prayers, followed by a trip to the Broch. Dad parted from them with all the praise, bonhomie and hearty handshakes usually lavished on his pupils. They promised to send him a bottle of the Bavarian equivalent of whisky - Himbeeregeist (raspberry spirit).

Afterwards, Dad endured much teasing about his new-found German friends and he blustered about them being Bavarians, Germany's equivalent of Highlanders.

Months later, back in Durham, deep into term time and all thought of German students forgotten, a mysterious parcel arrived. Inside was a bottle of clear liquid that tasted notionally of berries and burned an instant trail down the throat - Himbeeregeist.

Dad kept it for moments of acute stress, such as writing end-of-term reports or when both the gin and whisky had run out. He would raise a glass to his German students and cry, 'Ah, Himbeeregeist!' in fond memory.

Years later, in retirement, Mum finally got Dad to holiday in Germany. He loved it, of course.

Tigers and Yoga

After weeks on Skye, we would return to Scotland's capital and our grandparents' house in the solidly prosperous and respectable area of Murrayfield. Balnagown, with its whitewashed walls, elegant wide windows and veranda, stood out from the uniformity of solid stone-built villas and terraces, an Edwardian debutante among the Victorian matrons.

There was always an aspect of being in a time-warp at Balnagown. Forget the Sixties, it was still swinging from the Twenties, or at least mildly flapping. Granny Sydney, still slim and elegant and smoking aromatic Turkish cigarettes, had glamorous cousins who could have stepped straight out of a Scott Fitzgerald novel. They were witty and caustic and enlivened any parties - even tea parties - keeping us kids open-mouthed with their gossip. They talked with wonderfully deep, fruity voices that sounded of cocktails and Charlestons.

One had married someone very rich and become a Mosleyite. I had no idea what this meant, but by the tone of disapproval used to describe the condition, it was obviously dangerous - and possibly catching.

We were mesmerised by the Camerons, these flappers from another era. They were a frivolous antidote to Granddad's side of the family, the Gorries. Mum's Gorrie aunts were awe-inspiring; a powerful group of hard-working, unmarried suffragettes and campaigners. Aunties Bel, Mary and Beth had all been members of the radical Womens' Social and Political Union led by the charismatic Pankhursts, fighting for women to win the vote.

They had a courageous role model. Their mother, Janet, had rushed up to Winston Churchill (then in the pre-1914 Liberal Government which had consistently denied women the vote) and shaken her umbrella at him in public.

'Votes for Women, Mr Churchill!' she had cried, in a most demonstrative, un-Edinburgh way that could have got her arrested. He condescended to doff his hat and move on. One hopes that the incident had a lasting impression on Churchill, though the official history books don't relate.

But Janet Gorrie was used to life's rebuttals. She had been widowed young and left to bring up five children. It was a case of four-eggs-between-five economics. As the youngest, my Granddad always got the tops of the eggs. The three girls grew up knowing they would have to earn a living and sacrifices were made to put the eldest, Peter, through medical school. Janet was passionate about her 'bairns'. In fact she was passionate about most things, from emancipation to motorcars and would jump at the chance to ride in one - even the sidecar of Granddad's motorbike.

Janet's daughters were no less forthright. Bel, Mary and Beth had marched and demonstrated for women's suffrage. Bel sold copies of the suffragette newspaper, Votes for Women, on the street and was praised by the Pethwick-Lawrences for being their best seller in Scotland.

In 1909, they had taken part in a mass political rally, Bel dressed up as Mary Queen of Scots and Mary as Kate-Bar-the-Door, another Scots heroine. Beth was a leading light in Edinburgh University's Women's Suffrage Society. They appear to have taken an enthusiastic part in the Census protest of 1911, an act of civil disobedience that entailed staying away from home and partying through the night in an Edinburgh cafe, dressed up in fancy dress and lampooning various characters with false waxwork noses.

The vote won, Beth became a headmistress and a member of a women's club. Mary trained as a social worker and worked for the Scottish Female Domestic Servants' Benevolent Fund, campaigning on behalf of retired Scottish servants who had nowhere to live after a lifetime of working in other people's houses. The Gorrie aunts were generous, warm-hearted and deeply loyal.

Both sides of the family, only a generation further back, had come from rural Perthshire, the foothill to the Highlands. Janet Gorrie's father, Robert Maclagan, was the station master at Perth and a friend of Queen Victoria's infamous John Brown. The Camerons' father was minister at Logierait before dying young and necessitating his widow and young family's move to Edinburgh. His two young sons were sent off to Australia in the hopes of a better chance in life.

Jump back just one more generation and schoolmaster Samuel Cameron was a friend of Norman MacLeod, minister and eldest son of Donald of Suardal. In the way of the Highlands, my parents' families were connected long before they were born.

My granny appeared to be the lynchpin. Sydney was the quiet communicator, the World Service for far-flung relations. Maybe this stemmed from the days when she was exiled in India, the wife of a forester and kept in touch with family by letter. While Britain was shaking off the pall of the First World War, kicking up its heels and roaring into the Twenties, Granny took the long sea passage to India in 1923 to marry Bob Gorrie. Granddad had been inspired to work abroad by his admired elder brother, Peter, who had emigrated to Australia as a doctor.

But for Sydney, it was a life far removed from the comforts of Balnagown where she had grown-up, her interests in theatre and ballet, the parents who doted on their only daughter. Sydney trekked through the jungles of northern India with Bob, camped under canvass and organised supplies for the dozens of their entourage. When their daughter Sheila was born, she was carried in a basket by Sherpas through the foothills of the Himalayas, along with the provisions. They even trekked as far as Tibet on forestry projects.

Sheila's younger brother Duncan remembered being terrified by these treks in the Indian Hills.

'I was strapped on to a man's back in a basket then, when a bit older, on the back of a pony behind my father. One day the pony collapsed trying to climb up the bank from a stream and we fell off. There was too much weight. After that I had a mule of my own - and that was even more terrifying!'

They went for a month at a time and had to be self-contained, carrying everything with them - camping equipment and provisions - all of which Sydney had to organise.

Bob, a survivor from the trenches of Flanders and the second Battle of the Somme, was a man on a mission. He was a conservator of forests, passionate about trees, about tackling soil erosion and deforestation. He saw his role as training up his Indian students to take over from him when the British left, as that was the way he believed the future would go. Bob was energetic, quick-tempered and champed in frustration at the bureaucracy of British India. His appraisals from his superiors (now in the India Office of the British Museum) show their condescension.

'In the early years he was considered to have rather too high an opinion of himself and to require suppressing, but the passage of years has adjusted this.'

The Chief Conservator of Forests in the Punjab, a Mr G.R. Henniker-Gotley, praised him as "a tiger for work" and a very valuable officer, though "apt to ignore procedure and financial implications." While Financial Commissioner, Mr A.C. MacLeod summed him up more kindly as "Much travelled and full of ideas and energy, if somewhat impatient of the all-pervading red tape from which we all suffer."

Sydney, the peace-maker, often found herself in the role of 'smoothing ruffled feathers' after her impatient, idealistic husband had charged full-tilt at the fools he would not gladly suffer. Yet she too, at times, resented the high-handedness of the administrators and military who ran India and saw foresters as low on the social scale.

'The only time they showed us any attention,' she told her daughter dryly, 'was when they wanted your father's permission to go shooting or hunting in the forests.'

Granddad did not go shooting for pleasure. Perhaps two years of being a gunner in the Great War was more than enough for any lifetime. The only occasion he did so, was when called upon to rid an area of a tiger that had been attacking the inhabitants of several villages. He shot it dead. Mum remembers pacing out its entrails when the carcass was dismembered. The mounted head of this roaring beast hung in the hallway at Balnagown and was known as Gwendolyn.

At times, even long-suffering Sydney would lose patience with their itinerant life and catering for huge numbers in the jungle. Totally fed up on one occasion when another young forester was camping with them, she tried to stomp out in high dudgeon. But tents don't lend themselves to dramatic exits. She hit herself on the tent pole and ruined the whole effect.

116

Later, they had a more settled time in Lahore and my mother was joined by brothers, Duncan and Donald. Aged eight, Sheila was taken back to Scotland for schooling, looked after by her grandparents in Balnagown and fussed over by the kind Gorrie aunts. Sydney confided in a letter to her cousin Grace Cameron in Australia, "I love all my in-laws and am thoroughly envious of the children having such adoring aunts - I never had any, they were always dashed critical."

Sydney's mother, another Grace Cameron, was a loving and down-to-earth carer of her grandchildren. Duncan remembers being electrified when his grandmother bared her breast to him, telling him matter-of-factly that he should know what a woman looked like.

Just before the outbreak of the Second World War, Sydney came back to Edinburgh and did not see her husband for the next six years. Both her parents died early in the War but Balnagown remained the family home and Sydney never left it again. India gained independence but Bob remained in the employment of the Pakistan Government until the end of 1949 then, after a spell in Ceylon, came home too. By the time we were on the scene, the large house had been converted into three flats, my grandparents keeping the middle portion, along with the double garage and substantial part of the garden.

* * *

Arriving at Balnagown, we would race each other to the front door, arguing over whose turn it was to ring the bell. 'Hello Granddad!' I'd leap at him.

'Hello, my Jo-Janet,' he'd grin, parodying Burns and swinging me into the house.

Balnagown was a place of exoticness and ticking clocks. A jungle of plants grew out of massive oriental urns that stood on a wooden dais in the vast bay window of the high-ceilinged sitting-room. On the book shelves, among Tin-Tin and Barbar the Elephant in French, were blue china jars and a brass jug which we took down and played with. There were Chinese prints as well as family portraits.

It was a house of mystery and excitement with infinite choice for playing hide and seek; up by the plants or behind the large sofa by the clawed feet of the standard lamp, in the cool red-tiled cloakroom with curtains of gabardines smelling of Granddad or the pungent sanctuary of the pantry with streamers of onions brought by a Frenchman on a bicycle. Best of all was the secret balcony hidden behind a concealed and shuttered door. A curtain had to be drawn back, its birds of paradise collecting into folds, then the metal bar lifted to release the dark shutters and allow the unlocking of the final glass door.

From the balcony we could peer into the garden belonging to the flat below and across the high wall into the grounds of a spooky Addams Family-type mansion. We would sit on the faded swing-seat and rock back and forth until we felt queasy.

There was a cellar full of games; Spillikins and Bagatelle, dolls with hinged legs and waxy faces, boxes of old metal soldiers and miniature sandbags that had belonged to my uncles. The flat even had a room called the Captain's Cabin - Granddad's narrow study with a roll-top desk and lined with wooden cupboards like the fittings of a ship.

In here a truckle bed was erected in which I slept, once Angus had arrived and taken the berth in the camp-bed in Mum and Dad's bedroom. I was snug and shipshape, tucked into soft white linen sheets and quilt, guarded by old photographs of bearded ancestors and Granddad's certificate of commendation from the First World War hanging on the wall. 'Mentioned in Despatches' and signed by Winston Churchill (yes him again) now Minister at the War Office.

It seemed Churchill could track his career by reference to what my relations were doing. I imagined he paused while signing the certificate, nodding in appreciation. 'Gorrie? Edinburgh? Ah, must be Janet Gorrie's son. No wonder he showed such courage.'

While my parents were pampered by Granny with breakfast in bed, we would join Granddad for his early morning rituals of yoga and exercise. He would be almost naked, even in the chilly atmosphere of the cavernous sitting-room. His torso was white and sinewy, his neck and arms brown from gardening in the sun. As a small child I thought of these weathered limbs as the Indian bits of Granddad.

We lay on the Persian rug beside him and copied his movements with serious enthusiasm. Then he would lead us over to the raised dais and, with a book balanced on his head, jog up and down the three steps. Again we attempted to copy him like cartoon Mowglies from The Jungle Book, scattering books and making a great clatter on the wooden steps.

Three decades later, witnessing the arrival of Step aerobics to the British exercise scene, I thought of Granddad and his routine. He invented it. He was a man ahead of his time and the modern day versions are a pale imitation. Who else does Step among bowls of poinsettia with a volume of nineteenth century Scottish verse balanced perfectly on their heads?

After the morning puja would come breakfast in the dining-room, a warm place with its saffron-coloured carpet and wooden cupboards full of brightly patterned china, smelling of boiled sweets and starched linen. There was always porridge (made the night before) with cream, followed by toast and home-made marmalade or oatcakes and heather honey.

Granddad's picture grinned down at us from the wall, be-hatted and buccaneer, unshaven over his bowl of porridge. At least he told us it was him in his India days. Only years later did we realise it was a painting by Goya of some Spanish peasant and his bowl of soup.

* * *

After a prolonged spell in the Hebrides, trips into central Edinburgh to shop were a heady and alarming experience. For weeks, 'going down-town' had meant a visit to two shops, a post office and a garage. Now we practically had to relearn how to cross roads. We would take the bus from Roseburn up to Haymarket and the West End and get off at Princes Street to buy records and stand in the sound booths listening to the latest singles.

Sometimes one of us would need a kilt adjusting or a new one made and we would be taken to Forsyth's. If it was during the Edinburgh Festival, we'd be allowed to stand on the balcony overlooking Princes Street to watch the parade of pipe bands sweeping down from the Mound. Or we'd go to Jenner's, an exotic perfumed emporium, whose main attraction was to ride in the lift. I never tired of watching the uniformed guardian of the lift appear out of his lair with a flash of light and clash of collapsing metal as he concertina-ed the door of his cage to allow us in.

One time Granny took me all the way to the top, to the shoe department. She was going to buy me slippers for my birthday, not the most exciting of prospects, until she raised my hopes with a casual question.

'Would you like some boots?'

Would I like some boots! This was the era of boots - ankle boots, high boots, white patent leather and black suede boots. The Beatles had trendy black slip-ons. Nancy Sinatra was singing about walking all over someone in hers.

'Yes please,' I brightened.

We rode in the rattling lift, expectation mounting with the floors. It was short-lived. Granny led me over to the slipper selection and pointed at some fury slipper boots with zips, the kind her generation wore. She had not meant sexy boots after all. I struggled heroically to hide my disappointment. How could I explain that no self-respecting Beatles fan would be seen dead wearing old ladies' slippers even in the sanctuary of Jenner's shoe department? I settled for a pair of slip-ons instead.

* * *

There would be other pleasant trips laid on while in Edinburgh; Auntie Molly's in Corstorphine for home-made lemonade and games of Minister's Cat or Uncle Duncan's to play table tennis with our cousins, Alyson, Alastair and Jonathan. At New Year, Auntie Beth (the only one of the suffragist generation still alive) would treat us to a pantomime.

Mum, thwarted in her acting career, would snatch any opportunity to go to the theatre and to take us with her. Anything would do, from pantomime to Shakespeare, one-man shows to fully blown ballets. The frontiers of our theatre education were ruthlessly extended at the annual Edinburgh Festival where she booked tickets for everything from opera to late-night fringe reviews.

So it was, that when the infamous, hippy stage play 'Hair' came to town, Mum took us all to see it. We had heard about the nudity. My brothers couldn't believe their luck. It hardly lived up to the hype, but just before the close of the first half, the actors took off all their clothes (discretely and tastefully obscured by netting) and danced around the central character in the buff.

At the interval there was much excited talk about this closing scene.

Mum looked at us in bemusement. 'What nudity?' she asked.

We stared at her, dumbfounded. 'Mum! They all had their clothes off,' we cried.

She looked astonished. 'I was so intent on working out whether the person in the middle was a man or a woman, I didn't notice what the others were doing.'

'Mum, you are joking!' we cried impatiently.

'No,' she laughed in embarrassment.

It was probably the most iconic scene of the whole Permissive Society - and Mum had missed it.

'So was it a he or a she?' she asked as we took our seats again.

We rolled our eyes at her innocence. 'A man, of course!'

Often we were ungrateful at her attempts to introduce us to culture. She took us to the opera, Don Giovanni, and we grumped about the Italian.

'You complain about not hearing the lyrics in pop songs,' we protested, 'but what on earth are they on about?'

Yet other times, we saw productions that would fire our love of live performance for ever; a very Scots version of *The Comedy of Errors* at Murrayfield ice rink, *The Three Estates* performed in the Scottish Assembly on the Mound and John McGrath's polemic on Scottish history done as a ceilidh, *The Cheviot, the Stag and the Black, Black Oil.*

Living in Murrayfield, my grandparents' home was ideally positioned for entertaining large numbers of rugby supporters after Internationals at the Murrayfield Ground down the hill. Granny's rugby teas were famous. A large part of the afternoon would be taken up making dainty open sandwiches on rolls or crackers with fillings I had never seen before; dashes of black caviar on cream cheese, smoked salmon, strange toppings of lurid green called olives and gherkins.

We would squeeze among the legs of tweed and twill, handing round plates of sandwiches and cake, while Granny presided over an enormous Alice in Wonderland china teapot and Granddad poured drams for the frozen-fingered.

In the lull between trips out and entertainments in, we would amuse ourselves in the garden with games of cricket or racing round the washing poles until falling dizzy on the grass. The garage was a treasure house of earthy implements, thick washing rope and huge wooden pegs, tennis balls that had lost their bounce and a creaking rocking horse waiting patiently to be rescued from under its dust-sheet. We'd make up games in the summerhouse, opening faded doors to release the smell of warm canvas and dusty wood. From here we could see Granny picking fruit under netting in the vegetable garden, a slim figure in the sunshine bending with a basket over ruddy fruit. Whatever the game or adventure, Balnagown was always the haven to which we returned.

There was, however, one left-over element from old Edinburgh that we found less appealing. Into this Eden came Nanny Mercer. She was like one of the fierce-faced nannies in severe hats who queued up for a job in the film Mary Poppins only to be blown away in the wind for being too strict. Who was she? And why was she visited upon the third and fourth born of our generation? This was what Rory and I pondered as we peered at the sky for any signs of a change in the wind and Mary Poppins coming to our rescue.

It was only years later that I discovered she had been the nanny to the famous cricketer W.G. Grace's grandson, Hamish, whose father was a commander and presumably liked good discipline. The commander's mother-in-law was a Mrs Nimmo, a friend and near-neighbour of Granny's family in Murrayfield Drive. Mrs Nimmo had friends in high places because through her, my mother was presented at Court (Holyrood Palace to be exact) to Queen Mary and the young Princess Elizabeth.

Mum remembered every detail of that afternoon in 1947. She wore a red, white and blue dress and jacket and a blue bonnet made by Shwartz with flowers and red ribbon. The Princess had just become engaged and so, unofficially, had Mum (though Granddad was in denial and said it couldn't be official until she turned twenty-one). It poured with rain and Dad stood in the wet at the palace gates to see his fiancée go past.

The royal party walked around the room full of nervous young women and then Queen Mary stopped in front of the poised young actress, Sheila Gorrie. She admired Mum's hat at which stage Mrs Nimmo should have introduced her young charge. But Mrs Nimmo was so overcome by the encounter that she remained completely speechless and the moment was gone.

Shortly afterwards, Princess Elizabeth was pictured with a hat exactly like Sheila Gorrie's. Apparently, I too could have taken part in this strange ritual of the Ancien Regime and been presented at Court, for you can only be introduced by someone who has already been presented. Luckily in 1958, the year I was born, the custom of presenting debutantes was abolished and I was free to nurture my republican sympathies.

This was the background to Nanny Mercer. She came out of retirement especially for us. Presumably Granny thought it a kindness to give my parents a rest from us younger ones or maybe Granddad was attempting to stiffen the backbone of these pop-singing, boisterous urchins who regularly invaded the Eastern calm of his home.

Rory and I dreaded these walks with Nanny Mercer, when we were marched downhill with the sickly-sweet smell of the breweries in our nostrils. Afraid to speak, (for we never seemed to say the right thing) we walked like robotic children because moving in a spontaneous way - a hop, skip, jump or run - caused a sharp reprimand.

If we were very good, we were sometimes allowed to travel one stop on the local train as a treat. 'Very good' appeared to mean being as silent and briskly mechanical as possible. There was to be no unnecessary chattering, laughing, nose-picking, shoe-scuffing, sudden unexplained movement, nudging, shoving or breaking into Beatles songs.

So we marched around the unforgiving pavements of Murrayfield like those puppets on *Watch with Mother*, the *Wooden Tops*, crossing our fingers (in a way that didn't cause alarm) that we could go on the train and gagging on the subversive lyrics to *I Want to Hold Your Hand.*

Sometimes our efforts paid off and we got the longed-for one stop on the suburban line. What joy! Noise, steam, clanking, whistling, banging doors, a scramble for the window seat, bliss. We would gaze at the tenements, shops and depots flashing before our eyes, a field of sheep at the abattoir whizzing past too quickly. All our efforts were gobbled up in reverse.

Then it was a reluctant leaving of the warm seat for the final assault up the hill to Granny and Granddad's. Our tired legs would be spurred on by the thought of a Balnagown tea and being reunited with our long lost family. It felt like days since we had seen them, we explorers from the brewery-smelling Interior.

'We're back!' we'd cry, leaping at our bemused grandparents, with all the relief of shipwrecked survivors.

The general lack of surprise (from the grown-ups) or interest (from older brothers) was disappointing. Impossible to explain our euphoria to those who had not experienced our adventures at first hand. Yet our own bonds of comradeship in a shared campaign were forged for ever. With the relief of being home again and full of scones and cake, there was even an afterglow of wary respect for General Mercer.

The sense of awe and fear she inspired never dimmed with time. Even now, walking the speckled pavements of Murrayfield when the wind is blowing in a certain direction bringing the pungent smell of hops, my stomach can lurch. I'll visibly straighten, pick up my feet and fall into rhythmic step. Elderly passers-by nod in understanding and mumble, 'Ah, Nanny Mercer, Campaign of '62.'

Her legacy has also given me a life-long love of rail travel. Standing on a station platform watching in anticipation as a train pulls in, still gives me a thrill quite disproportionate to the event.

And Rory? He joined the army and has marched through deserts and jungles. Nanny Mercer would have been proud. She certainly deserves some credit for preparing him for active service.

From Pimlico to Carnaby Street

The world changed in 1968. Revolution stirred. The barricades went up in Paris, the students sat down in the US against Vietnam and the MacLeods moved out of The Caffinites. Although the event went unmentioned in the national press, the repercussions were seismic. Dad's tenure as housemaster was over. He was to continue as a history teacher and move into a smaller school house.

While the parents got on with packing and throwing out fifteen years' worth of family junk, we were dispatched to stay with Uncle Donald and Auntie Astrid in Limekilns, Fife. We had a happy time playing football with cousins Robert and Euan and challenging the local boys in a field overlooking the north shore of the Firth of Forth. Auntie Astrid fed us well. At some point we were collected and taken north to Skye for the rest of the summer holidays as usual. But when we returned to Durham, everything had changed.

Mysteriously, our Beatles pics did not survive the move. Dad's wind-up gramophone disappeared too. And most unsettling of all, Don suddenly grew up and left to go and live on the other side of the world in Papua New Guinea about which we knew absolutely nothing. He was to work for a year at a Franciscan mission in Koki, a pioneer of the now routine 'gap' year for students. Bereft, Mum and Dad tried to cheer themselves up by playing his Leonard Cohen records, which of course had completely the opposite effect. Cohen's tortured, angst-ridden lyrics about Suzanne taking him down to the river, only served to remind us all that Don was not there to take us anywhere.

The secret gardens and cavernous hide-and-seek house of Caffinites was now out of bounds, home to new housemaster, Nick Gedye and his family. Gazing up the driveway, we saw our football pitch fenced off and reclaimed as a garden, slowly reviving under gardener George's tender fingers. The next time I visited, the downstairs rooms had been redecorated in modern greys and everything had shrunk. I was Gulliver among Lilliputian corridors and hallways that had once seemed so vast and never-ending.

We moved to Number Two, Pimlico. Technically, it was just across the street - less than a hundred yards away - but we had moved worlds. Pimlico was a dog-leg terrace of red-brick houses, like a huddle of humble academics squeezed between Durham School and the riverbanks, gazing rather enviously across at the venerable Cathedral and the prestigious University colleges.

The house we were to occupy had been lived in by an elderly lady who used to sit in the upstairs bay window with the sole purpose (we thought) of spying and informing on us. If she saw us heading off down the street without an adult, she would contact our parents. With the benefit of hindsight, Mrs Thursfield was obviously the type of concerned neighbour that every parent wants, but to us her interference was an early form of ASBO (Anti Social Behaviour Order). Pimlico for us meant a quick dash down the street, breath held and eyes averted from the bay window of Number Two in the hope that Mrs Thursfield would not see us.

Number Two was tall and thin - a John Cleese of a house - handsome arched windows on the outside, unstable and wobbly within. Later, it was discovered to have no foundations. Like a biblical reflection of my parents' financial acumen, it was built on shifting sands.

Cracks appeared in the outside walls at the back of the house, so glass plates were reassuringly inserted to measure any further shift. Gradually, daylight could be seen through the crack in my bedroom wall and when I had a nightmare about being tipped into the backyard, the school arranged for two cheerful Irish labourers to come in and shore up the house.

The school also paid towards the decorating of the house when we moved in. When my parents retired in 1985 they were still mostly living with the same 1968 wallpaper. Our bedrooms were a time-warp of Sixties swirls or childish knights in armour that we had chosen as children. I lived in a psychedelic heaven of orange walls, turquoise carpet, orange curtains and a small armchair upholstered in orange. To wake in the morning (not an option of choice for a teenager) was made magical by the morning light filtering through orange cloth and projecting onto orange walls. The whole room was bathed in a tangerine glow.

It was a warm, south-facing room with a view over the clutter of Pimlico backyards to a wedge of wilderness between two roads with noisy rooks in the tall trees. In summer, the distant school buildings disappeared behind green leaves and the air thrummed to the sound of wood pigeons. Big Puss, our hard-bitten tramp of a cat, liked to lie on the hot pipes that ran under the floor by the window.

As toddlers, Rory and I had staggered into Caffinites clutching the tabby cat we had found outside and plonked her down. Mum, hating cats, promptly put her out. But she was a stray, chased away from the neighbouring house by territorial dogs and we retrieved her. Big Puss stayed and abused our hospitality. She had countless casual affairs, produced litters in Dad's sock drawer, fought, scratched and bit her way through life. No one messed with her except at their peril. At first, Big Puss thought little of down-sizing to Pimlico or swapping the jungles of Caffinites' grounds for a one-flowerbed backyard. She came on occasional visits. But when a cat-flap was put in the back door, regular meals lay waiting in the small kitchen, and she discovered that not only was the house centrally heated but the despised backyard was a suntrap, she deigned to move in with us.

Big Puss grew old there disgracefully. Her craftiest trick was to tear the fabric of the sofa with her sharp claws - a hideous sound - to indicate that she needed to leave the room. Then as soon as someone got up from watching the TV to let her out, she would neatly side-step their legs and leap into the empty seat. We fell for it every time. She grew bronchial and dribbled. She sounded like a motorbike revving up when she purred. Big Puss lived at least nineteen years, liking nothing better in her old age than to plonk herself down on the letter Mum was trying to write or the council papers she was trying to read. But long ago, this bruiser of a cat had butted her way into Mum's heart and it was Mum who missed her the most when Big Puss closed her suspicious green eyes for the last time and died.

With Don away doing voluntary work overseas and Torq in Scotland at boarding school, the scales of the household tipped in favour of the female for the first time. Mum took in lodgers - four women from Neville's Cross teacher training college who took up residence in the attic. These students personalised their study bedrooms with hippy bedspreads and cushions and the bathroom clothes-dry dripped with exotic accessories such as nylon tights.

Mum gave them a cooked breakfast every morning, carried up on trays. The smell of over-done bacon would seep into my consciousness from the kitchen below. Then she would breeze into my room with Big Puss at her heels and pull back the curtains.

'It's a lovely sunny morning,' Mum would announce, or say something poetic about the state of the clouds, the trees or the likelihood of rain. In another life she was probably a Celtic bard.

I never appreciated this morning lyricism or the fact that both my parents could be so cheerful this early. It took all my effort to grunt that, yes I was awake, and flail with a limp arm until I hit the right button on my new transistor radio. Radio One's Dave Lee Travis and a blare of music would dowse me like cold water and bring me round. Thirty years later, of course, I was doing it to my own beloved sleepy-headed children and sounding like the weather forecast.

'It's a lovely morning,' I would lie, pulling back the curtains. 'Bit cloudy, but no rain.'

Something would stir under the duvet and mumble incoherently about not caring. That day they might not. But just give them thirty years.

* * *

As the Seventies dawned in Pimlico, Cindy and Tressy dolls in their groovy Sixties clothes were still played with, but they had been joined by Paul, Cindy's trendy boyfriend. With students in the attic to observe, and visitors tramping up and downstairs, relationships suddenly became more fascinating. Tressy, the fearsomely busty and leggy blonde with hair that extended by pressing a button in her stomach, needed a boyfriend too. I cast around and came up with the rather desperate solution of Angus's Action Man. His wardrobe was pretty limited - khaki and camouflage - but he could borrow something of Paul's.

'Do you want to come and play in my room?' I asked Angus sweetly. 'You can bring Action Man.'

It worked. Action Man was lured out of his lair (a rather secretive bedroom tucked away beyond the bathroom) and into the room of tangerine dreams. But it didn't take this highly trained operator long to realise it was a girlish trap. As soon as Action Man realised he was on a blind date with the busty blonde, his taut plastic muscles went rigid.

'I'm not playing with Tressy,' he said in disgust. Within seconds Action Man was sprung to freedom in SAS style.

The girls and Paul pursued him back to his hideout. In desperation, Action Man leapt for the open window. Without a backward glance, he was out on the window ledge and then before their startled eyes, took a death-defying jump into the abyss (the backyard). Cindy and her friends stood in vexation, yet a little in awe of the lengths Action Man would go not to socialise with them. It was the last time they pulled a stunt like that.

Afterwards, they languished more and more in their box of dated clothing, until finally relegated to that dusty forgotten place on top of the wardrobe, waiting for time (and the next generation) to bring them back into fashion.

Just as Pimlico was becoming familiar and seeming more like home than Caffinites, the time was approaching when I would be leaving it for the bracing sea breezes and spartan living of convent boarding school in Whitby.

Mum and I made a trip to Harrogate to buy school uniform from the only shop that sold the green and buff finery that was St Hilda's trademark. Thankfully, a new tunic had just been introduced. No longer did pupils have to wear the St Trinian's style bib and flared skirt of the past fifty years. Neither was it compulsory to wear the dark green, pudding-basin felt hats with elastic chin strap. Cindy and Tressy wouldn't have been seen dead in them.

However, there were strange and complicated items on the long list of essentials. White knicker-linings to go under voluminous dark green pants. Stockings and suspenders. I'm sure there was mention of a corset.

Middle-aged women with tape measures fussed around us.

'No,' I hissed through clenched teeth, 'not suspenders.'

'But it says here ... ' Mum tried half-heartedly.

'No!'

We came away with several pairs of fawn socks and suspenders were never mentioned again. A trunk was bought and a sewing basket. Name tapes were ordered. I chose purple ones and watched Mum sewing them onto my buff blouses and green jumper with mounting dread.

But there was a family tradition that helped sweeten the pill of impending separation. The rite of passage began with a special weekend away with a parent. Mum had taken thirteen year-old Don to Paris before he went to Strathallan School in Perthshire. Three years later, Dad had taken Torq to

London. So it was Mum's turn to take eleven year-old me to the big city.

London, 1969: The Beatles were still the Beatles, the Sixties were still Swinging - just - and I was going to the Capital for the very first time.

We stayed with friends in Hammersmith, a connection through the chiefly family on Skye. The Zveginzovs were 'White' Russians, a baffling phrase at the time, but I knew it was something to do with being opposite to Communist Red. To this day, my favourite film is *Dr Zhivago* and its tale of romance in the upheaval of the Russian Bolshevik Revolution. Omar Sharif, the actor who played Zhivago, was soon to be pinned up on my orange wall, and here I was going to stay with real Russians.

They lived in a tall rambling terraced house with a garden going down to the River Thames. It was stuffed with books and old furniture, untidy and cerebral, welcoming but with that distracted air of the academic. Michael was cheerful, Diana languid. Both were kind and full of conversation. But what gave the whole place that extra Gothic frisson was the knowledge that they had a strange son who dwelled in the attic.

I had heard about Alexander; Torq had been frightened by him three years previously. Alexander liked to stay in his room, but I wasn't to worry about meeting him (which made me worry about meeting him). By the time I did, I was in a frenzy of anticipation and dread. He didn't disappoint. His mother took me up to see him. He was a grown man, tall and looming, with close-cropped hair who stared at me like someone from a Hammer Horror film. I was electrified.

I think I said something brave like, hello. Then he spoke, not directly at me, but to his mother. Out of this hulk of a man came a high-pitched, childlike voice. A gentle giant. He didn't seem so frightening after all. A few years later he would come and stay at Suardal where we all grew fond of him. Yet at the time, to sleep in this bohemian house in the heart of London and hear Alexander moving about in the room above, was more exciting than *Jane Eyre*.

Over the next three days, we got down to some serious sightseeing. Mum was in her element. She had lived in London during the Forties while studying drama at RADA and knew her way around the tube network, the West End and the sights. We whooshed around underground and emerged at one landmark place after another. The Tower of London, Big Ben, Carnaby Street (at my request) with its jaunty stalls and union jack clothing. I got to see the Beatles (if only as wax-works in Madame Tussaud's). She took me to see Agatha Christie's *The Mouse Trap*, at the theatre and I crowed at the end of the evening for having guessed who-done-it.

But this was London, the mecca of pop and fashion. I hankered after a leather jacket. We embarked on a morning shopping trip that trailed on into the afternoon in a fruitless quest for a jacket that would fit me. From Sloane Square to Oxford Street we searched. Even Mum's energy flagged. The most we had ever shopped before was the occasional foray into Newcastle.

But usually something garish from C&A satisfied the urge. In the end, we returned to one of the first shops we had visited and bought a dark leather waistcoat that I had tried on at the beginning of the day, when Mum had uttered the fatal words, 'Let's see what else there is first...'

We retreated to a flat in Cheyne Place, Chelsea, belonging to Dame Flora's family. The house had been built by her husband and requisitioned during the Second World War to accommodate bombed-out families. Newly renovated and turned into flats, we were to have tea there before going to the theatre. It was then I discovered Mum collapsed on the floor of the bedroom, her legs sticking stiffly in the air against a stool. The world stopped. I had killed my mother with shopping.

Engulfed in guilt and panic, I flew across the room. 'Mum!'

She opened her eyes. 'I'm just resting,' she said rather accusingly.

'Why are you on the floor?'

'It helps tired legs if you raise them above your head,' she explained.

'Oh.'

The world juddered into life again, but I was chastened. Too much shopping was bad for you, or at least for your mother. My interest in it as an activity waned from that moment onwards.

There was someone else with a Russian connection in London whom I met for the first time. We went to have lunch with an old school friend of Granny Sydney's, Doreen Stanford. Mum had lived with her while studying in London over twenty years before. Doreen was a retired secretary, small and plump with fluffy white hair and an engaging chuckle. No one would guess that as a teenager, Doreen had lived in remotest Siberia in a wooden house with a huge samovar, snowbound through the long winter, while her father worked as an engineer in the local mine.

Even less would they believe that Doreen and her parents had fled before the advancing Bolsheviks, caught up in the chaos of thousands of others fleeing by troika, ferry and train. She witnessed and never forgot, some woman screaming for her child who had been left behind on the riverbank as the overloaded ferry pulled away. She met a Czech soldier who had guarded the Tsar's family and claimed to have a note written by one of them. He was taking it with him, a keepsake that he could sell if he ever escaped to America.

Doreen and her parents managed to reach Vladivostok in the East and onto a ship, eventually making it back to Europe. They arrived in Edinburgh, penniless and had to split up and find work where they could. Doreen stayed with her old school-friend, my grandmother. Fifty years later, Doreen still had huge Russian banknotes from the Tsarist regime that were worthless and small photos of a land of sun and snow where she had lived briefly, but happily.

So, Mum and I, alternated between these parallel London worlds. The bustling, brash, touristy city of Beafeaters, red buses and Beatlemania; and the hidden world of exiles behind the gentile facades of Victorian terraces.

I returned, heady from the experience, wearing a green Paisley-patterned blouse with my new waistcoat still smelling of leather. I wore them with my faux-leather mini skirt from C&A, and even though they didn't match, I felt as trendy and with-it as anyone who walked the King's Road.

That summer Don came home. We waited for his arrival, excited yet nervous at what we might find. The year felt like a life-time. When he walked through the door of Pimlico, we gawped at this half-stranger. He was thin-faced with a straggly beard and wearing a dark hat or cap. We embraced him almost shyly and listened in wonder to his traveller's tales. He had journeyed back from far New Guinea via the USSR and sold his jeans in Moscow to some underground Beatnik. (Don was soon to go to Oxford and become a Communist, but I can't help feeling those jeans were probably the beat of the butterfly's wings that started the counter-revolution of Glasnost twenty years later).

And I was going to the Anglican convent in Whitby. I was leaving Durham behind and all the things I casually took for granted; my orange room, brothers, a walk into town to buy records, central heating, schoolboys, Big Puss, TV, Mum's Fruit Fool, cycling with Helen, Dad's jokes, Mum's humming. Kissing them goodnight.

In the September, my sophisticated leathers were packed into my new blue trunk alongside the virgin uniform. Neither I nor my swinging waistcoat was prepared for the culture shock soon in store for us both. I said goodbye to Dad and the brothers who were still at home - Rory, my childhood playmate and Angus, who was turning into a good mimic and made me laugh with his Steptoe impersonations. I couldn't eat the final meal for my stomach was plunging up and down like the lift in Jenner's Department Store.

Mum drove me south and over the Yorkshire Moors, taking the old pilgrim's route out of Durham where the Cathedral comes into view for the first time. Except we were heading in the opposite direction - away from monks and my life among males - towards an extraordinary life among schoolgirls and nuns.

My childhood home, my childhood town, receded from view through the back window and was gone.

Lightning Source UK Ltd.
Milton Keynes UK
UKHW010949281220
376014UK00001B/167